W9-BMG-334

# QUILT
## with the
# BEST

Edited by
CAROL COOK HAGOOD

Oxmoor
House®

*To Amanda and Emily,*
*Rebekah and Kathryn,*
*and all the quilters*
*of the century ahead.*

Library of Congress Catalog Number: 91-68146
ISBN:0-8487-1078-9
Manufactured in the United States of America
First Printing 1992

Executive Editor: Nancy J. Fitzpatrick
Director of Manufacturing: Jerry Higdon
Art Director: James Boone
Copy Chief: Mary Jean Haddin

*Quilt with the Best*

Editor: Carol Cook Hagood
Assistant Editor: Lelia Gray Neil
Designer: Earl Freedle
Senior Photographer: John O'Hagan
Photostylist: Katie Stoddard
Patterns and Illustrations: Karen Tindall Tillery,
Larry Hunter, Melissa Jones Clark
Assistant Copy Editor: Susan Smith Cheatham
Production Manager: Rick Litton
Associate Production Manager: Theresa L. Beste
Production Assistant: Pam Bullock

# Contents

## CHERYL GREIDER BRADKIN

Quilters across the country have
learned to make colorful mosa-
ics of Seminole patchwork from
Cheryl Greider Bradkin's books,
articles, and workshops. Now she
shows how to incorporate Seminole patchwork designs into
sweat-fleece play clothes the
whole family will enjoy.

## AMI SIMMS

It's the essential skill for quilters:
joining the layers of top, batting,
and backing with small, even
stitches. Most quilters would like
to improve their technique: Ami
Simms offers good advice on tools
and materials and a step-by-step
demonstration of the quilting
stitch.

# Introduction

Picture a year spent in the company of quilting greats like Helen Kelley, Jan Myers-Newbury, Cheryl Greider Bradkin, Flavin Glover, and the other master quilters featured in this book. That's the unique opportunity that the staff of *Quilt with the Best* enjoyed this past year, as we traveled across this country and abroad to bring you stories of some of the finest quilt teachers at work today. It was our privilege to watch—and record—as eight extraordinary craftswomen shared their expertise with groups of eager students, or guided us through special demonstrations set up just for you, the *Quilt with the Best* reader.

In May, we journeyed to the magnificent Wind River Mountains of Wyoming to meet quilter, potter, and stained-glass maker Marta Amundson. Her rich, jewel-like quilts, accented with striking animal quilting designs, are powerful statements of her concern for environmental issues. Animal designs also appear in her stained glass and pottery.

June brought a visit with Merikay Waldvogel at the historic Ramsey House in Knoxville, Tennessee. Merikay's work with the Tennessee State Quilt Survey is an instance of the ongoing grassroots efforts of today's quilters to document and celebrate our quilting heritage. Merikay offered insights on quilt history and gave some helpful guidelines to use in dating antique quilts.

In July, we followed Helen Kelley, known to thousands of quilters through her monthly column, "Loose Threads," in *Quilter's Newsletter Magazine,* to a week-long quilter's seminar on the lovely Isle of Arran, off the west coast of Scotland. Commenting on the growth of interest in quilting around the world, Helen says that enthusiasm for the craft is "spreading like wildfire." We were pleased to watch as this great American quilter shared her expertise in ribbonwork, a reverse appliqué technique based on a Native American design tradition, with a congenial group of quilt enthusiasts from Scotland, England, and Wales. In the photographs, you will get a glimpse of the beautiful countryside of Scotland and of Park House, a very special quilter's retreat you may wish to visit.

All through the spring and summer, we welcomed notable quilters from across the country to our home studios in Birmingham, Alabama. Californian Cheryl Greider Bradkin brought her knowledge of Seminole patchwork and some tips for working in popular sweat-fleece fabrics. Margaret J. Miller, from Woodinville, Washington, demonstrated her amazing formula for transforming traditional patchwork patterns into striking new designs. She also explained her exciting color strategies.

From Flint, Michigan, Ami Simms brought detailed instructions for improving our quilting stitches (along with great stories and more than a laugh or two). Flavin Glover, from Auburn, Alabama, surprised us with a new way of working with Log Cabin patchwork, translating the traditional Tumbling Blocks pattern into a showstopper Log Cabin quilt.

Jan Myers-Newbury, celebrated quilt artist from Pittsburgh, Pennsylvania, showed us how easy and enjoyable it really is to hand-dye fabric in gradated color sequences and how these gradated fabrics can be used to achieve dramatic effects of light and movement in our quilts.

And, of course, all these gifted quiltmakers brought *quilts*—extraordinary, breathtaking quilts—which we are delighted to share with you in these pages. In addition to the solid, practical information presented in step-by-step workshop photos, each of these dynamic teachers, through her quilts and the story of her career in quilting, offers a spark of creative energy—an invitation to catch the flame of excitement that burns so brilliantly in her own work.

After a fascinating year, it's our pleasure to bring you this quilt-conference-in-a-book. We hope you will enjoy *Quilt with the Best* and that it will open the door to delightful new challenges in your quilting. We welcome your suggestions of other fine quilting teachers whose work you would like to see featured in the pages of Oxmoor House publications and invite your comments on how we can be of service as you continue to grow in this craft. Please write to us at this address:

Editor
Quilt with the Best
Oxmoor House, Inc.
2100 Lakeshore Drive
Birmingham, AL 35209

# Seminole Strips: Patchwork at Play

When quilters think of Seminole patchwork techniques, one name that springs quickly to mind is that of Cheryl Greider Bradkin. Cheryl has been teaching the techniques of Seminole patchwork since 1978. Her first two books on the subject were a hand-lettered volume, self-published in 1978, followed by a color version in 1980. These books introduced many quilters to this popular style of quilting, with its colorful strip-pieced bands based on the traditional patchwork made by the Seminole Indians.

In August 1991, Cheryl's new book, *Basic Seminole Patchwork* (Leone Publications), appeared as a replacement for the 1980 title. In this new volume, Cheryl shares up-to-date directions for the basics of the technique. Quilters will find how-tos for over 60 Seminole patchwork designs—including new graphed mosaic flower designs—and guidelines for quilts, towels, totes, and quilted clothing.

"I first became interested in Seminole patchwork in 1977," Cheryl says. "I was at a crafts fair and saw a man wearing a shirt that had Seminole patchwork in it. I knew the name of the patchwork but had no idea how I knew it. Later, I remembered that my mother, who collects and wears ethnic clothing, had a skirt made by Seminole Indians, and that is where I had first seen the technique used. I studied that skirt—which she still has—and tried to figure out how the patchwork was done. It took some

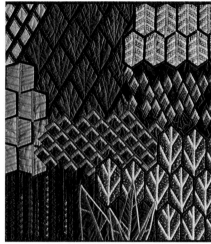

*Jungle,* Detail

library research. This was in 1977; there was a revival of interest in quilting, spurred by the Bicentennial. I found one really thick book on quilting, and in that entire book, one page on Seminole patchwork—but that was enough to show me how to make the strip sets and then offset the pieces."

Then she researched photographs of Seminole patchwork in *National Geographic.* She studied

---

*I like creative clutter; I have an inspirational bulletin board just covered with things. But I also like to have some organization—I have this thing about boxes and containers. Seminole patchwork is very methodical, and I do like that.*

---

and sketched the designs from the Indian garments and tried to figure out how to make each one. "In making mistakes while trying to make *those* designs," says Cheryl, "I discovered still others. Indian women have thousands of variations that they sew."

Cheryl, who has a degree in zoology from the University of California at Berkeley and who has worked as a biologist, found that Seminole patchwork happily combined the precision important in her scientific background with her love of color and textiles. "I am drawn to Seminole patchwork because it is so orderly," she says. "In my life, I seem very disorganized. I like creative clutter; I have an inspirational bulletin board just covered with things. But I also like to have some organization—I have this thing about boxes and containers. Seminole patchwork is very methodical, and I do like that."

Also, she adds, when you take Seminole to the point that she does—making mosaic designs of quarter-inch squares, for example—it can require very fine handwork, like that needed for the work she did in biology or for other needlework that she enjoys, including Aran Isle knitting, with its complex patterns. But Seminole patchwork can also be very simple.

This agreeable range of complexity is reflected in the workshops that Cheryl most often teaches, which include *Basic Seminole Patchwork, Stitching the Seminole*

*Sweatshirt,* and *Creative Seminole Piecing.* In the third workshop, Cheryl explains, "We explore the possibilities of making Seminole patchwork look like leaves, waves, feathers, and such. It's a fun class, and I enjoy getting to see other people's ideas of how to use the technique."

In her own work—whether quilted wall hangings or one-of-a-kind garments, like the five she has designed for the Fairfield/Concord fashion shows that highlight Houston's annual International Quilt Festival—themes are likely to be botanical or zoological, and her favorite color is green. Not just one green is favored, however, but a spectrum of greens, chosen from a fabric collection developed over time. "I like to use fabrics from different years and therefore from different palettes; it's more exciting to have yellow-greens and blue-greens and gray-greens mixed together than to have all shades of, say, blue-green. For some years, you couldn't find any good yellow-greens; now they are available again. For variety, I pull colors from my fabric stash, a 16-foot wall with shelves all the way to the 8-foot ceiling."

In stocking her stash, Cheryl looks not only for variety in colors, but for prints that offer interesting textures. "I like very tiny prints, prints that look like a lively solid from a distance. I also look for normal, broadcloth-weight fabric that looks like it has a texture. Heavyweight fabrics can be difficult to use in Seminole patchwork, but a broadcloth printed to look like a denim or burlap can have exciting possibilities. And sometimes, I even purposely check mill-end tables for misprints; misprints can be very interesting."

In putting this wealth of fabric to work, Cheryl takes a relaxed, low-key approach, insisting that her patchwork is to be enjoyed every day, here and now: "My quilts are wall pieces and I hang them, like paintings, all through our home. I don't worry about fading, and I don't worry about whether they're going to last for generations, because they are just for me and for my family and our immediate pleasure. I have the same attitude about clothing. The one-of-a-kind special pieces that I do are worn very rarely and I don't worry

about how difficult they are to care for. But I also enjoy making easy-care patchwork that can be worn to the grocery store. That's the nice thing about the Seminole sweatshirts—they're so easy to make and easy to care for. They're a really good example of patchwork to live in."

*Tsukiji Market* 37" x 46" 1987

The *Tsukiji Market* quilt is a result of a teaching trip to Japan in 1986. While I was there, I took lots of slides of the food in the open-air market; it was all so beautifully displayed in wooden boxes. When I got home and was looking at my slides, I realized that these boxes, with the vegetables, almost made quilt blocks. So I started designing Seminole patchwork vegetables and used the designs to make this quilt.

At the time, I thought this vegetable patchwork was something entirely new for me. Later I remembered that, years ago, Georgia Bonesteel had asked me to do a block of my house in Seminole patchwork for a program she was doing on quilters' homes in patchwork. In that block, in the backyard of the house, I had a done a little summer garden with Seminole patchwork lettuce, tomatoes, and corn. But that was as far as I had gone with the vegetable designs until I did *Tsukiji Market.*

Our favorite vacation spot is a hot beach with good snorkeling. My husband teaches college math and engineering. During the semester break that comes each January, we like to go to the beach. I made this quilt for our bedroom. When I wake up in the morning, I see that beach and the fish in the water and for a few seconds I think, "Now, am I in Tahiti, or am I in Sacramento?"

Also, I wanted to explore using Seminole patchwork to make the trunks and the fronds of the palm trees. The fish were an obvious kind of thing to do with the basic element of Seminole design: that little square on point.

*Island*
31" x 44"
1988

In *Jungle*, I wanted to use Seminole patchwork to do blocks with irregular edges. Essentially, the blocks are overlapping and topstitched—that's the way I kept the irregular edge.

This quilt is, I suppose, my environmental piece. In the machine quilting, there are images of animals—feet and stripes and feathers and things—meant to express my concern about the clear-cutting of forest land all over the earth. We're worried about the tropical forests, but in the Pacific Northwest, forests are also being clear-cut and animals are disappearing because of it.

Green is my favorite color. I think everything I have ever done has green in it somewhere, because of my love of nature.

*Jungle*
43" x 30"
1989

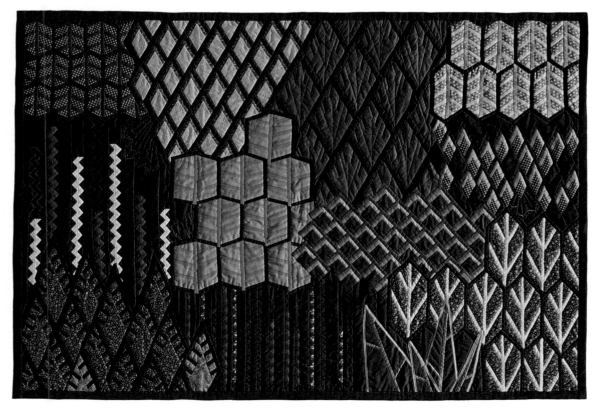

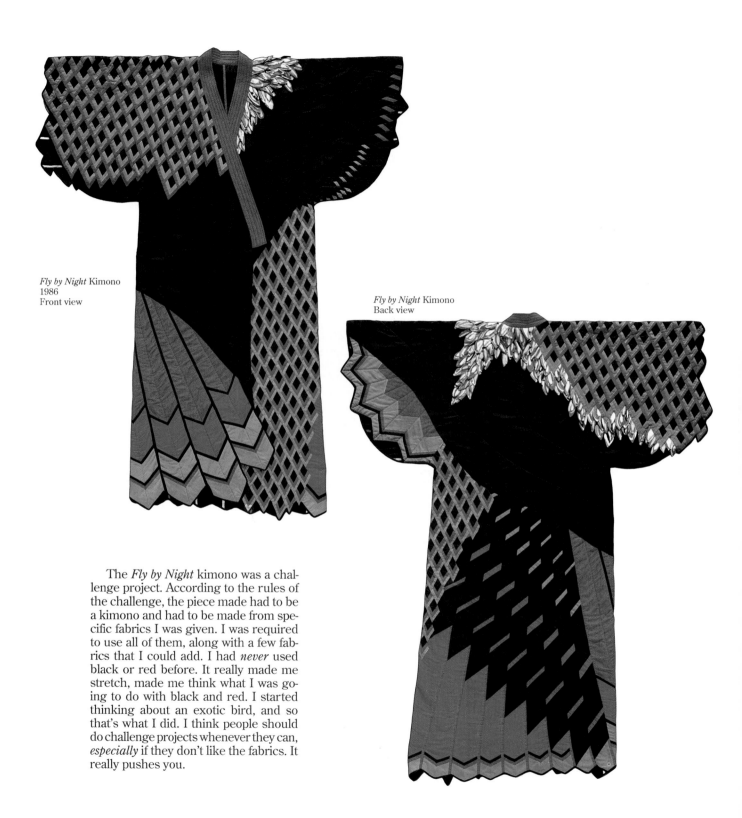

*Fly by Night* Kimono
1986
Front view

*Fly by Night* Kimono
Back view

The *Fly by Night* kimono was a challenge project. According to the rules of the challenge, the piece made had to be a kimono and had to be made from specific fabrics I was given. I was required to use all of them, along with a few fabrics that I could add. I had *never* used black or red before. It really made me stretch, made me think what I was going to do with black and red. I started thinking about an exotic bird, and so that's what I did. I think people should do challenge projects whenever they can, *especially* if they don't like the fabrics. It really pushes you.

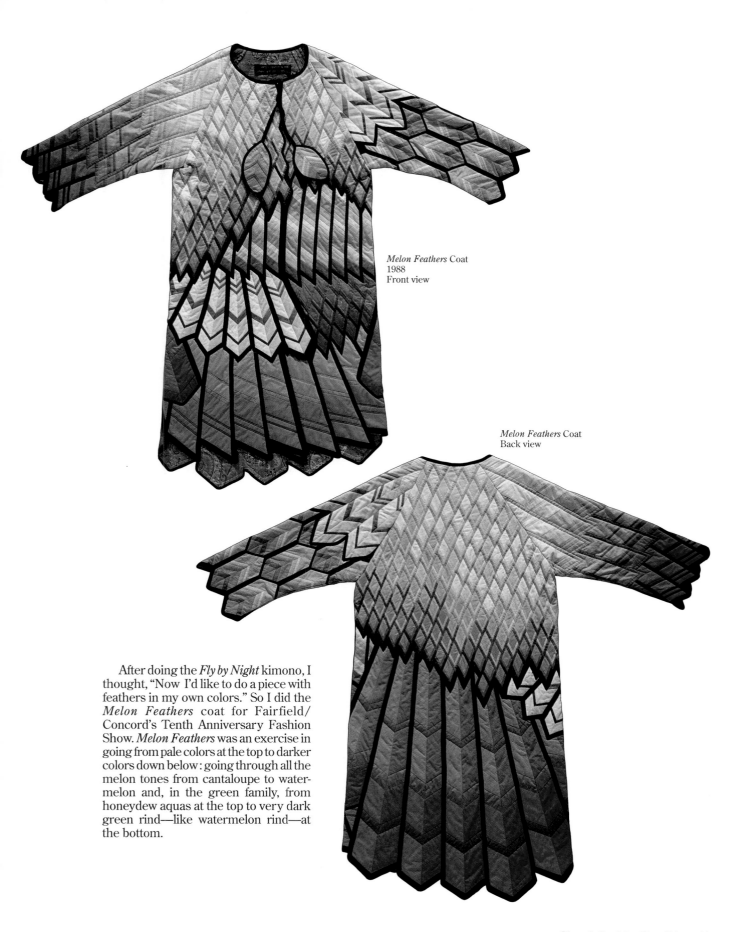

*Melon Feathers* Coat
1988
Front view

*Melon Feathers* Coat
Back view

After doing the *Fly by Night* kimono, I thought, "Now I'd like to do a piece with feathers in my own colors." So I did the *Melon Feathers* coat for Fairfield/Concord's Tenth Anniversary Fashion Show. *Melon Feathers* was an exercise in going from pale colors at the top to darker colors down below: going through all the melon tones from cantaloupe to watermelon and, in the green family, from honeydew aquas at the top to very dark green rind—like watermelon rind—at the bottom.

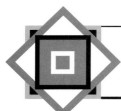
# Stitching Seminole Sweatshirts with Cheryl Greider Bradkin

Cheryl Bradkin's quilts include hangings with wonderfully intricate piecing and dramatic, one-of-a-kind garments. But, in her warm and easy-going manner, she reminds us that patchwork pleasures are not limited to such spectacular productions—or even to the light- to mediumweight cottons quilters most often choose for their projects.

As she demonstrates to students in her popular "Seminole Sweatshirt" class, shared in the following pages, exciting patchwork designs can be worked in colorful, comfortable, easy-to-wear sweat-fleece fabrics. In a few hours' time, students can make handsome patchwork garments to use and enjoy every day. When adapting Seminole patchwork designs to sweat-fleece fabrics, here are some important points to keep in mind:

• Preshrink all fabrics. Preshrinking, required in all patchwork, is especially important when working with knit fabrics. And consider using cotton-and-polyester or acrylic blends. The higher the cotton content of the fabric, the more shrinkage can be expected.

• For minimum stretch, cut the long strips required along the lengthwise grain of the fabric.

• Strips should be cut no less than 1" wide. (The strips will measure ½" finished).

• To help move bulky fabric through the sewing machine, use a seam ripper or orange stick as a "pusher." But take care: Never use the ripper or other pusher near the needle.

• Press seam allowances open to evenly distribute the heavy fabrics.

• When pressing the garment during construction or after laundering, be careful not to stretch the patchwork design out of shape. Use a steam iron and a light pressing technique. (Press straight down; never push the iron along the surface of the patchwork). After pressing, allow the fabric to cool completely before the garment is moved.

Once you have mastered patchwork in sweat fleece, Cheryl suggests that you try your hand at other knit garments, like the T-shirt she wears in the following pages, or a patchwork-trimmed T-shirt dress. Lighterweight knits are admittedly trickier to work with, she says—especially jerseys, which tend to curl; choose interlock knits for more stability. But for your *first* adventures in patchwork knits, Cheryl advises that you use the heavier sweat-fleece fabrics. They're easier to handle, she tells us, and much more forgiving.

**Gather Materials and Tools**

You'll need to assemble the following items:

Sewing machine with a new size-80 or size-14 needle. Set stitch length at 10-12 stitches per inch. Place a seam allowance guide made from charting or masking tape on the bed of your sewing machine, exactly ¼ inch to the right of your sewing machine needle. (The edge of the presser foot is not a reliable guide for sewing sweat fleece, because of the fabric's thickness.)

Steam iron

Rotary cutter and mat

Transparent plastic ruler with printed grid lines

Fabric scissors

Thin soap sliver to use as a marker

Pins

Seam ripper or orange stick

Ready-to-wear sweatshirt–either dropped-shoulder or raglan style. Choose a 50% cotton/50% polyester or acrylic blend to minimize shrinkage and look for a straight grain on the front of the shirt, especially on the left side where the patchwork band will be inserted. Prewash and dry.

½ yard each of 3 sweat-fleece fabrics, of any fiber content. To unify patchwork and shirt, 1 color selected should match the shirt as closely as possible. Prewash and dry.

1 (135-yard) spool of thread to match sweatshirt.

## Make Patchwork Band

The colors of sweat-fleece fabrics you choose will determine the personality of your Seminole sweatshirt—bright and contrasting colors for an attention-grabbing shirt or subtler colors for a more reserved design. To unify the patchwork and the shirt, 1 color should match the shirt as closely as possible. In the photograph at right, the pink fabric is very close to the color of the shirt; but even fabrics that don't precisely match can work well, because the "matching" fabric will be separated from the shirt by the other colors, and the eye will tend to "read" the shirt and the "matching" fabric as the same.

If you are uncertain about your choice of colors, make a fabric mockup of a portion of the patchwork design; this will be of greater help to you than just looking at yardage colors together.

Using your rotary cutter and mat, and with the gridded plastic ruler as a guide, cut 1 (2½-inch-wide) strip each of blue and purple—the outer colors—and 1 (1½-inch-wide) strip of pink—the center color. (*Note*: These measurements include ¼-inch seam allowances.) To minimize stretch in the strips, cut with the lengthwise grain of the fabrics; each strip will be about 18 inches long. Cut a single layer of fabric at a time and align the edge of the ruler cutting guide with a rib of the knit loops in the fabric.

Join blue, pink, and purple strips with ¼-inch seams into an 18-inch-long striped band or *strip set*. (After sewing the first 6 inches, check the seam to see if the thread tension or

presser foot require adjustment. If the seam is gathered, reduce thread tension. If the seam is stretched, reduce pressure on the presser foot.) With the steam iron on the permanent press setting, press seam allowances open. Press first on the wrong side of the strip set and then on the right side until the strip set is straight and flat.

The sweatshirt will require 2 (18-inch-long) strip sets, so make a second strip set just like the first.

With the rotary cutter, cut strip sets apart into 1½-inch-wide pieces. To make straight cuts, keep the short grid lines of the ruler parallel to the seam lines of the strip set. (*Note:* Very thick sweat-fleece fabrics—generally, those with high cotton content—will create bulkier seams. To keep the Seminole patchwork design true, you may have to make each piece just a little bit larger to allow for this extra bulk. If your fabric is especially heavy, add 1/16 inch to the width of each piece as it is cut from the strip set.)

Arrange the cut pieces in pairs, turning every other piece upside down and offsetting so that the central pink squares align, with corners touching. (If a single piece is left over, discard it.) Join each pair together with a ¼-inch seam. (Use thread to match shirt. We have used a contrasting thread here so that seams will be more visible in the photos.)

*Note:* For speed and thread economy, use chain sewing, or continuous seaming, as you sew the pieces together. When all the pairs are joined, clip across the chain to separate the pairs.

Lay the pairs out, again offsetting, as above. Blue and purple will alternate position from piece to piece. Join pairs together to make a completed patchwork band.

*Note:* As you join pieces into pairs and pairs into a patchwork band, you are sewing with the direction of maximum fabric stretch. If the pieces begin to stretch as they pass between the presser foot and the feed dogs, push the fabrics along with the point of a seam ripper or orange stick (never working too close to the needle).

When the patchwork band is completed, it will have slanted ends at top and bottom. Straighten them in this way: Make a straight cut across the band through the center of any pink square. (See diagrams.) Then sew the slanted ends together in the offset position. You now have a completed band of patchwork with straight ends at top and bottom. Press the band flat from the right side, letting the seam allowances go in the direction they fall. If the design becomes distorted, gently push the design back into shape while the fabric is hot and let cool before moving it.

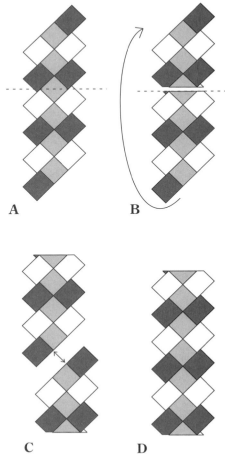

A          B

C          D

Trim away the long, jagged side edges of the band. Place the ruler on the band as shown, with the long grid line ½ inch in from the ruler's edge positioned at the outer points of the pink squares. Cut along the edge of the ruler. Trim the second long side of the band in the same way, checking to be sure that both cuts are parallel, so that the band is an even width all along its length.

Trim the top end of the band ¼ inch above the top point of the last complete pink square. Use the gridded ruler to make the cut at right angles to the long edges of the band.

Confirm that the finished patchwork band is as long as the front of the shirt from the shoulder crease to the top of the waist ribbing.

### Mark Sweatshirt

Lay the sweatshirt out flat. Pinning the shirt onto an ironing board, if possible, stretch the left front waist ribbing to straighten the area in which the patchwork band will be inset. Steaming the ribbing may help to relax it.

Place the patchwork band on the left side of the sweatshirt without stretching the band. The top of the band should extend beyond the shoulder crease ½ inch. (For a dropped shoulder style, place the top of the band even with the shoulder seam.) The band should be about ¾ inch from the neck ribbing and should lie parallel to the grain of the knit of the sweatshirt (unless the shirt was cut off-grain).

Trim the bottom of the patchwork band even with the seam line between the shirt and the waist ribbing.

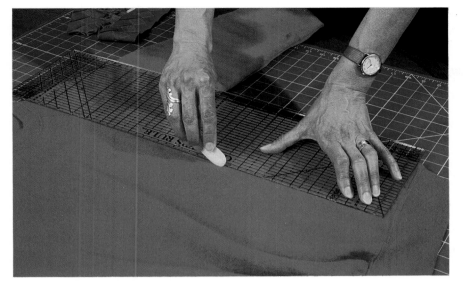

Carefully measure the width of the patchwork band. Use a narrow sliver of soap to mark a placement rectangle on the sweatshirt. (Avoid soaps with cold cream that may leave a greasy stain.) Begin the first vertical line ¾ inch from the neckline ribbing at the shoulder crease. Using the ruler and following the grain of the shirt, extend the line to ½ inch above the ribbing at the shirt bottom. Mark a second vertical line parallel to the first and at a distance from the first equal to the width of the patchwork band minus 1 inch.

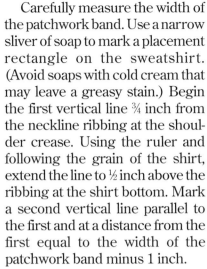

The top line of the placement rectangle, connecting the 2 vertical lines, should be marked, as shown, at the shoulder crease on a raglan-style sweatshirt. (On a dropped-shoulder sweatshirt, mark the top line ½ inch below the shoulder seam.) The bottom line of the placement rectangle should be marked ½ inch above the waist ribbing.

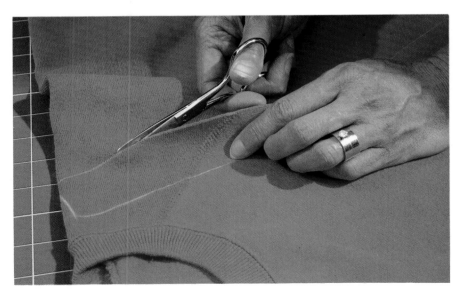

Cut along the marked lines with sharp scissors, taking care not to overcut at the corners and not to stretch the cut edges.

## Stitch Patchwork to Shirt

The long, outside edge of the opening cut in the sweatshirt is the edge most vulnerable to stretching, so stitch the patchwork band to this edge first to stabilize the opening. Pin the long outside edge of the patchwork band to the long outside edge of the opening, right sides facing. The ends of the band should extend beyond the ends of the opening ½ inch at the top and ½ inch at the bottom. At the top and the bottom of the band, place pins at the midpoints of these extensions to show where the seam should begin and end.

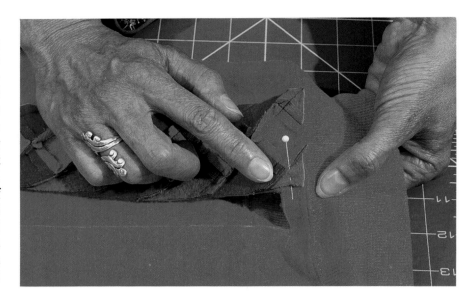

Sew the long outer edge with a ¼-inch seam, stitching from pin to pin.

Turn the shirt wrong side out to pin the long inner edge of the patchwork band to the shirt opening, with right sides facing. Turn the shirt right side out to check that both long vertical seam lines are smooth and even. Turn the shirt wrong side out again and sew the second long seam.

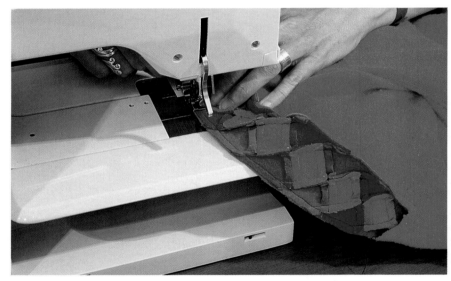

Before sewing the ends of the patchwork band to the ends of the opening, make a diagonal clip from each corner of the opening halfway to the point at which the vertical seam line ends. Do not make the clips any deeper than this: The sweat-fleece fabric is very stretchy, and you need to avoid making any holes in the finished seam.

Sew the ends of the patchwork band to the ends of the opening, using ¼-inch seams and connecting the ends of the long seams. Turn the sweatshirt right side out and use a steam setting to press the patchwork band flat.

Your Seminole sweatshirt is ready to wear! The sweat-fleece fabrics will not ravel, so this special sweatshirt requires no more care than an ordinary one. Do take care not to overdry the shirt in a dryer, as most sweatshirts will continue to shrink with every drying.

Photograph by Melissa Springer

## Patchwork for Everyone

Now that you know the techniques needed to work Seminole patchwork in sweat-fleece fabrics, it's time to share the fun. With a little thought and experimentation, you can make patchwork-trimmed playwear to please the whole family. Any simple Seminole design can be used to make the patchwork accent. *Note:* As a guideline, a decorative band for adult sweatpants requires 3 (18-inch-long) strip sets. Choose a pants style without pockets or begin the band just below the pocket.

# Quilt Adventures with Ami

Ami Simms quilts with silver thimbles of her own making. Before she began making them, she had searched the world—a good bit of it, anyway—for the kind of thimbles she wanted: strong, metal ones with deep, well-defined dimples on the top, to help hold needles securely and offer real control over the quilting stitch. When she was unable to find thimbles that pleased her, Ami registered for a course in metal casting at the Flint Institute of Arts so that she could make her own. First, she had to convince the reluctant instructor that a serious thimble maker had a place in the class. Then she went to work learning the lost wax process to make her thimbles.

The other students carved wax models of the silver objects they wished to make and surrounded the models with plaster of paris molding material; tubes of wax ran from the model through the mold to the outside. When the molds were heated, the wax models and tubes burned away. Then molten silver could be forced, using a centrifuge, into the molds, filling the space originally occupied by the wax models, to make the silver objects desired. Ami followed the same process as the rest of the class, but instead of wax models, her molds contained plastic thimbles, imported from England and marked with lovely, deep indentations all over the top.

When the molds were heated, the plastic melted and ran from the molds, leaving an impression ready for a fine silver thimble. By experimenting, Ami found that she could decorate a thimble by dribbling melted wax on the plastic thimble before placing it in a mold. She could even personalize a thimble with her initials, by gluing on tiny vinyl letters from an office supply store.

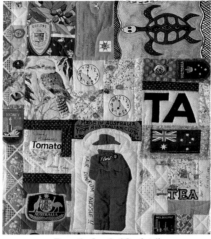

*From the Land of Oz,* detail

*If you disagree with an expert, remember, there are no experts: You have to find your own way. Your own enjoyment is the bottom line. There are enough have-tos and shoulds in life.*

The letters, too, burned away during the melting process.

Ami's thimbles are lovely to look at. (You'll see one at work—close up—on the following pages.) What's more, they tell a lot about the qualities that this quilter brings to her quiltmaking: self-reliance, ingenuity, and an energetic willingness to find her own path to successful quilting. Though Ami's introduction to quilting took place in the most traditional setting imaginable (at an Amish quilting bee she attended as part of her research for an honors thesis in anthropology), her early quiltmaking was almost entirely self-taught. She acknowledges that she made many mistakes. Her first quilts were quilted with an embroidery needle (a needle is a needle is a needle, she figured) and no thimble at all. Only after several years and several quilts did she attend a national show, where an examination of the prizewinning quilts acquainted her with some of the finer points, such as matching seams and smoothly stitched bindings.

The long list of award-winning quilts Ami has since produced attests to her increasing proficiency and mastery of the craft. She enjoys thinking back over her quilts and remembering the lessons each taught. In one piece, for example, she learned appliqué; in another, she used a thinner batting and found that she could make much smaller stitches; in yet another, she perfected rotary cutting. And she values the freedom she enjoyed in learning from experience. "If I were a beginner in this day and age when there are so many teachers, workshops, and classes, I don't know if I would have continued. It can get pretty intimidating!" Instead, by making her own mistakes and learning from them,

Ami developed well-earned confidence.

Her "can-do" attitude has led Ami into some unusual projects that might never have occured to the less adventurous. In 1983, she and her friend Mary Blandford decided to make signature quilts bearing the embroidered autographs of celebrities from many walks of life. At the time, Ami was teaching geography, history, and current events at several senior citizens' centers and nursing homes; she encouraged her students to nominate people to contact for autographs. In time, she and Mary had collected over 200 pieces of muslin signed by luminaries, including Isaac Asimov, Joe Dimaggio, Paul Newman, Lucille Ball, B.F. Skinner, Marcel Marceau, Indira Gandhi, and Milton Berle. Ami used her autographs to make an 89-inch-square geometric patchwork quilt. She included 30 different calico prints in brown, rust, blue, and green to give a scrap-bag effect and to reflect the very different achievements of the notables who had contributed their autographs. The quilt is accompanied by two 10-pound companion notebooks of correspondence surrounding the project, including a few treasured refusals—*three* of them from Katharine Hepburn.

While the signature quilt may be Ami's most novel piece, her many other quilts are marked by a variety of style and content that shows the same spirit of adventure. Refusing to be boxed in to one particular type of quilt, she has tried her hand at many different styles. Her pictorial quilts reflect scenes from her actual and "armchair" travels, including scenes from the Amish heartland. She enjoys making reproduction Amish quilts, doing traditional layered block appliqué, and experimenting with string quilting and quick machine assembly techniques. Patchwork garments are another favorite type of project. "I receive influences from all over," she says. "I will never run out of ideas!" Many of Ami's treatments of traditional themes reflect her keen sense of humor: A fabric self-portrait becomes *Woman With Fly On Nose*; the old favorite Sailboat pattern reappears, nose-down, in *Sinking Sailboat*.

Since 1982, Ami has shared her special blend of quilt wit and wisdom with thousands of students in classes coast to coast and abroad (in Holland, Australia, New Zealand, England, and Canada). In addition to providing solid, practical information, it's important to Ami that her classes be entertaining. "I want people to come into my workshops and have a good time. I want their experience in my class to be really enjoyable as well as challenging."

It's essential, she believes, that quilters keep their sense of fun and declare their own creative freedom: "My advice to my students is to ignore what anyone tells you, on any subject at all, and do what you darn well feel like doing as long as it pleases you. If you disagree with an expert, remember, there are no experts. You have to find your own way. Your own enjoyment is the bottom line, not pleasing a quilt judge, or your friends, or turning your quilting into a chore by having to crank out quilts for everyone and his uncle. There are enough have-tos and shoulds in life."

Luckily, Ami's good advice, good humor, and solid, useful information are available not only through her classes but through many publications. She has been a contributing editor to *Quilt*, and her work has appeared in various other publications, including *Great American Quilts 1988* (published by Oxmoor House), which featured her *Whig Rose* quilt as its cover design. In addition, Ami operates her own publishing house, Mallery Press, which has produced the popular titles *Invisible Appliqué, How to Improve Your Quilting Stitch, Every Trick in the Book,* and a new book, *Classic Quilts: Patchwork Designs from Ancient Rome.* In this latest book, ancient Roman mosaic floors are translated into exciting new quilt designs.

In the future, it seems likely that Ami's energy and ingenuity will continue to lead her quilting in many directions at once. "I must have a zillion projects going at any one time," she says, "and I work on whatever I'm feeling most passionate about at the moment. I like handwork, but I enjoy machine work, too. And the speed of machine work makes it possible to be a little more experimental. If you work on a machine-stitched project for two weeks and it turns out that you don't like it, fine. Go try something else. There's not the same investment that you have in a hand-stitched piece."

When Ami visited with us in the summer of 1991, she was working on a new piece that contains both hand piecing (using her "invisible appliqué" technique) and machine piecing—the *Confetti* quilt for her new book *Classic Quilts*. (Photographs on preceding pages show Ami putting *Confetti* in the frame for quilting. On this page, you see the finished quilt.) "I want to continue to grow in my quilting; I'd like to do more experimental things like the border of the *Confetti* quilt. I realize that I am obsessed with symmetry in design, and I want to test moving away from that."

It's a good bet, though, that Ami won't be moving away from quilting any time soon—or from her frenetic schedule of designing, quilting, publishing, traveling, and teaching. "I'm tickled with what I'm doing," she says. "I wouldn't trade with anybody. I'm doing exactly what I want to do—I just wish there were more days in the year!"

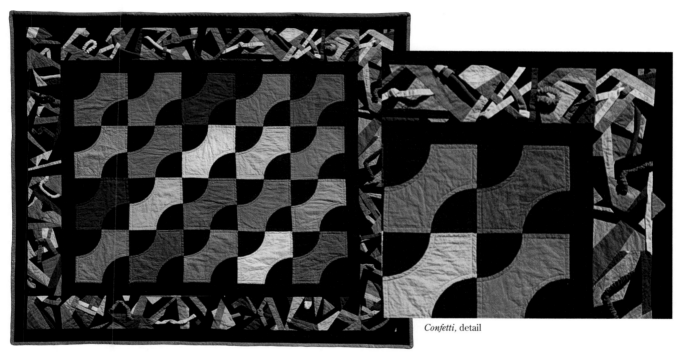

*Confetti*, detail

*Confetti*
44" x 37"
1991

## CONFETTI

This quilt, *Confetti*, is from my new book, *Classic Quilts: Patchwork Designs from Ancient Rome*. The block pattern for the interior of the quilt is called Nero's Fiddle.

I picked the colors for the quilt by working with the print fabric used for the backing. (See the second photograph in this chapter, where I'm putting the backing into the quilt frame.) Since I don't have any formal color training, I appreciate good ways to "cheat" with color. One easy way to establish a color scheme for a quilt is to find a print fabric you really like and pull colors from the print for the piecework. The added bonus to this method is that you get to use the print for the quilt backing, to pull everything together.

The border of this quilt was really fun to do, even though it took three times as long to do as the quilt's interior—and *that's*

hand-stitched. I used random crazy-piecing with dimensional effects, a combination of techniques that was new for me.

I have taught a string-piecing class for a long time, and in that workshop we talk about ways of embellishing the strings, like folding a piece of fabric and tucking the raw edges into the seams, or inserting prairie points into the seams. I thought, "Why not make a series of tubes and then try to weave the tubes in and out of the pieces, too?" After reading an article on trapunto techniques by John Flynn in *Threads* Magazine, I borrowed the idea of stuffing the tubes by using a needle and thread to pull yarn through them. So I had these flat tubes and these stuffed ones. And then, when I had just one piece of yarn left, I thought, "What if I just pull the yarn to gather the tube?" Then I got these wormy pieces—my favorites. I had a great time with this border.

*St. Basil's Cathedral*
48" x 63"
1989

## St. Basil's Cathedral

*St. Basil's Cathedral* is my most recent pictorial quilt. It contains more than 1,300 pieces of 100-percent-cotton hand-dyed fabrics. (I hand-dyed all the fabric except for the gold lamé and two funny-looking greens.) The quilt is stitched together using my invisible appliqué technique, stitching one fabric piece to the next. I don't use a muslin or other fabric base. Instead, I use a full-size paper pattern and transfer the sewing lines from the paper pattern to the fabrics, using a light box.

This quilt has been selected for use in a series of greeting cards by World Contacts Network, a nonprofit organization that pairs pen pals from North America and former Eastern-bloc countries. *St. Basil's Cathedral* has also appeared in *Quilter's Newsletter Magazine.*

I have never been to the Soviet Union; in making this design, I worked from photographs. My mother brought me the three Russian coins that are sewn to the top of the tallest tower. She had made a visit to the Soviet Union while I was stitching the quilt. It took about three years to make this quilt, but I did other things during that time, too. (I wrote my books *Invisible Appliqué* and *Every Trick in the Book*, and I think I cleaned the oven once.)

## HAPPY NEW YEAR!

This quilt was the subject of a Winter 1990 article in *Quilt* magazine in which I tell how I finally learned to use my rotary cutter. (For a long time, I think I was the only teacher on the national quilt circuit who didn't use one.)

With the end-of-the-year inventory of unused fabric looming ahead, I finally found the courage to slice up my fabric with the rotary cutter and get it into a quilt—and once I got the hang of it, I was hooked.

I named the quilt *Happy New Year!* because I was relieved at not having to inventory my entire fabric stash and because I was really happy to learn rotary cutting. There would be no more "true confessions" at my next string-quilting workshop about my lack of expertise with this popular tool.

The pattern for this quilt is taken from an antique quilt I found hanging in a furniture store in my home-town of Flint, Michigan. The original quilt has bright yellow circles that seem to float above all sorts of fabrics of the thirties.

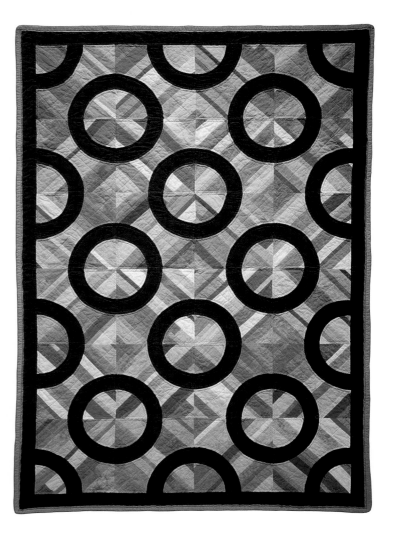

*Happy New Year!*
40" x 58"
1989

## PURPLE PINWHEELS

Many of my quilts are made with hand-dyed fabric. An article by Jan Myers-Newbury in *American Quilter* magazine was one of the pieces that got me started experimenting with hand-dyeing. Then Judy Walters's book helped me an incredible amount. Now I use a still different method: I don't even know its correct name—I call it "Ami's mottled mess." My 50-yard bolt of muslin comes rolled on a tube that I suspend from the rafters in my basement. I pretreat enough fabric for one dyeing; then it goes right into the dye and right out—that fast. I jam it into a plastic bag and toss it on the basement floor to cure for 24 hours, giving it a special mottled effect.

For years after I began dyeing fabric, I couldn't bear to cut into any of it, even though I had yards and yards, because then I wouldn't have it any more! All this fabric was sitting there, and I would go caress it, touch it, and love it, and I'd think, "I should really do something with this someday." Then I'd think, "Nahhh. If I cut it up, I'll probably never be able to make more just like it." (Since I know I'm going to like whatever color I dye, I don't go about it scientifically the way most dyers do. I don't keep track of dyeing formulas and have no real desire to duplicate fabrics. Creating one-of-a-kind yardage is more fun.)

Finally, after a long time, I got up the nerve and the desire to cut into my dyed fabrics. I made this piece, which I call *Purple Pinwheels*, for my mother. She's my best friend, and she deserved it. This piece makes use of seven or eight gradations of purple fabric.

Once you've quilted with hand-dyed fabric, you really get spoiled. It has a sueded texture that feels *so darn good*—it helps curb my appetite for commercially produced fabrics. (Well, sort of.)

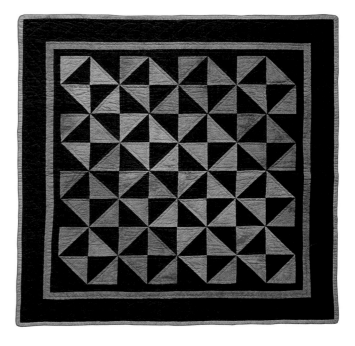

*Purple Pinwheels*
32" x 32"
1988

*From the Land of Oz*
45" x 33½"
1990

## FROM THE LAND OF OZ

*From the Land of Oz* is a memory quilt. In September 1990, I was fortunate enough to teach in Australia at the Australasian Quilter's Symposium. Other American teachers there were Jeana Kimball, Harriet Hargrave, Margaret Miller, and Marsha McCloskey. Marsha and I challenged one another to make a quilt during our visit. Our quilts had to be made from fabric obtained in Australia, and the top had to be finished during our two-week stay. (During this time we also planned to teach a full schedule of classes, attend dinners, luncheons, fashion shows, and all that—*and* try to see a bit of the country!)

As the students got wind of our project, they began to come to us at workshops and meals with little bits of Australian fabric and lapel pins, little patches, little this, little that. It was great! On my first shopping trip, I'd bought some Aeroplane Jelly Crystals—a gelatin like our Jello—for my daughter Jennie, thinking that we'd enjoy making a treat together after my return home. One of the students came in with fabric that had Australian products printed on it, and the first one was this Aeroplane Jelly Crystals block. Marsha and I fed Arnotts Biscuits to the kangaroos, so the inclusion of that block of preprinted fabric was a natural. There is fabric with designs drawn by an Australian woman who attended the conference;

fabric with little clocks on it to signify the 13-hour time difference; and a knife, fork, and spoon to remind me of all the Australian foods we ate. There's even a tiny music box inside the quilt. One of Jennie's toy animal souvenirs received a "kangaroo-ectomy" in the lunch line one day so that my quilt could play "Waltzing Matilda."

Marsha taught a class on working with the color yellow, so she had lots of yellow prints and solids with her; after her class was over, I bagged her leftovers. All the Australian teachers contributed something, too. Pauline Rogers won the fashion show; there's a patch of the silk fabric used for her winning garment, along with her name tag. Jen Luck taught machine embroidery; she contributed an embroidered patch.

What fun! I am normally a very planned quilter. I draw designs on paper first. I talk to the quilt; it doesn't talk to me. I tell it exactly what I want it to do. This quilt had a mind of its own. I had no pattern, no idea of where the next piece of fabric was coming from—let alone where I would sew it. I had no pins to sew with, didn't prewash the fabric—just slopped the piece together on borrowed machines, let it grow wherever it wanted to, and had an absolute ball putting it together. I came home with a finished top and quilted it, free form, on the machine.

# Improving Your Quilting Stitch with Ami Simms

For most quilters, improving the hand-quilting stitch is an important aim. No matter what the project, be it large or small, simple or complex, old-fashioned or as up-to-the minute as today's news, it's not a quilt until its layers are joined with quilting. And while machine quilting is a good alternative for some pieces, there remains a tremendous interest in hand quilting. Small, even stitches are the goal.

Ami Simms has shared her ideas on quilting with thousands of quilters in seminars across the nation and abroad, in magazine articles, and in the pages of her book, *How to Improve Your Quilting Stitch*. (For more information on this or her other books, you can write to Ami at Mallery Press, 4206 Sheraton Drive, Flint, MI 48532.)

On the following pages, Ami gives pointers from her workshop and demonstrates the quilting stitch as she has taught it to her many students.

### Check Your Quilting Environment

As the first step toward improving your quilting stitch, you should take a look at all the variables (other than the quilting stitch itself) that influence quilting performance. From the wide array of materials and tools available to today's quilter, you need to make informed choices.

*Fabric selection* is your first important decision. Quilters today use many types of fabric to get the effects they want, but for small, even quilting stitches, the fabric of choice is good-quality 100-percent cotton. Hold fabrics up to the light; generally, the less light you can see through the fabric, the better the quality. Be sure to prewash fabrics to remove any finishes. (*Note:* Before prewashing, clip a small triangle off each corner of the piece of fabric to limit raveling.)

The backing for your quilt should be 100-percent cotton, also. Don't use bed sheets, because they are not always 100-percent cotton and are difficult to pierce with the needle in any case.

*Batting* is your second important decision. Generally, the thinner the batting, the smaller the quilting stitch—unless you're using cotton. Cotton battings are flat, but generally are more difficult to pierce with the needle than synthethics and require more closely spaced quilting lines to keep the batting layer from shifting.

However, ease of quilting is only the first consideration when you're choosing a batting; you also need to think about long-range performance. Some synthetic battings can present a problem over time with "bearding," or the migration of batting fibers through the quilt top and back.

My recommendation is that you test samples of the different types of batting available to find the one that suits your own needs best. Using fabric like that you intend to use in your quilt and a variety of battings, test each sample for needle-ability by joining the layers with hand quilting. Then test for durability by sandwiching a 6-inch sample of each of your favorite batts within the proposed quilt fabric. Machine-quilt it and bind the edges. Then put the miniquilts through 2 machine-washing cycles. Check for bearding, pilling, bunching, and shifting. You might never plan to wash your finished quilt in the machine, but this treatment may give some indication of how your quilt will behave over years of gentler care.

*A frame or hoop* is required to keep the basted quilt layers at the proper tension for quilting. I use a floor frame made of 1 x 2s and C-clamps, held on custom-made metal legs that are adjustable, so that the frame can be positioned at different heights for basting and quilting.

A hoop can also be used. Choose one that is supported, so that it will hold the quilt for you, letting you concentrate on your quilting stitches. One quilting hoop I recommend can be ordered from The Frame Mate, P.O. Box 26964, Tempe, AZ 85282. Write for more information.

*Needles* should be short and sturdy for making small stitches. The higher the number, the shorter the needle and, more importantly, the *thinner* the needle is. The thinner the needle, the less resistance it will meet as it passes through the fabric sandwich. Experiment to find the shortest needle you can comfortably use and to determine the difference it makes in your stitching.

*Thimbles* are essential. The best quilting tool you can get yourself is a thimble with deep indentations on the top; good indentations are necessary so that you can "park" the needle in the thimble and use the thimble to control the quilting stitch. One of the most useful thimbles you can buy in this country has a criss-cross pattern of ridges resembling a tic-tac-toe pattern on the top surface.

Other choices, in addition to tools and materials, come into play in analyzing your quilting environment:
Your *quilting strategy* plays an important part in determining how difficult it will be for you to make small, even stitches. Quilting near or across seams is more difficult because you must deal with the extra bulk of the seam allowances. Quilting in-the-ditch (along the seam line) is also difficult for this reason. Outlining seamed pieces by quilting just beyond the seam allowance or quilting in "no man's land" (that is, in the open areas between seams) is easier.
Quilting on the bias is easier than quilting along the

grain line of the fabric. This may be one reason for the huge amount of diagonal cross-hatching in antique quilts. Once you start that straight-line quilting on the bias, it's so much fun you just don't want to stop.

Direction of quilting is important, too. For right-handed quilters, right to left is generally easier, and the reverse is true for left-handed quilters. For everyone, it's generally easier to quilt toward the body than away. I use a swivel chair on wheels so that I can easily turn my body in relation to a new quilting direction. With time and practice, you will learn to stitch with greater ease even if it's not your favorite direction.

Simple, straight-line quilting designs are easier to quilt than more elaborate designs because they usually require less starting and stopping. They are also less interesting, though, so there is a trade-off.

Your surroundings are vital as well. You need a good source of *direct, focused light.* (You should be able to see the light reflect off the tip of the needle as it emerges from the quilt.) I use an architect's lamp and adjust the focus of the light each time I change the direction of quilting.

Even the *weather* has a strong effect on your quilting. You know that if the air is damp your hair becomes fluffier. So do the fibers of your quilt. And moisture on your hands can make your needles oxidize, which makes them harder to push through the fabric. If you note discoloration, or oxidation, on your needle, pitch it and start again with a bright, new one.

Finally, your inner climate has a lot to do with how easily you can make small, even stitches. *Experience* is a key word; the more practice at quilting you have, the better you are likely to do. And your *mood* makes a big difference, too. If you're feeling confident, your quilting is likely to go well. (That's really the point of checking all the other variables: By making your quilting life as easy as possible, you are setting yourself up for success.) If, however, your mental outlook isn't at its best ("I can't do anything right. My husband's mad at me. We haven't had a home-cooked meal for three nights in a row.")—that's bound to show up in your stitches.

In other words, if your quilting doesn't quite come up to the standards you're looking for, *it's never your fault!* In my theory of creative scapegoating, there are always plenty of other factors you can point to. (And, with the pressure off, you can go right back to enjoying your quilting, which will probably make it improve.)

## Now Look at Your Stitching

When you've checked all the variables that can help create the best environment for your quilting, it's time to work on the quilting stitch itself. You need to make sure you are handling the needle in the way most likely to produce good stitches.

Let's start with the basics: To get small, even stitches, *the needle must enter the quilt in a vertical position.* (That's right: straight up and down!) Many quilters don't make the needle enter the quilt vertically, because they are handling the needle with their index finger and thumb, as in regular sewing. That almost guarantees that the needle will enter the quilt at an angle, making the stitch on the back smaller than the stitch on the top. In the quilting method I teach, the needle is manuevered with a thimble worn on the middle finger; as you'll see, this makes it possible for the needle to enter the quilt in a perfectly vertical postion. Second, for relatively painless stitches, the bottom finger must not push the needle back up too soon. Many quilters let the needle go too far through the quilt and push up sooner than they should. I'll show you how to feel the needle just as it exits the quilt and how to push it up at the right time, so that the stitch will be tiny and even and your finger will not be pricked.

In the photographs that follow, the quilting stitch is broken down into a series of steps; with practice these steps will flow together into fluid movement.

*Practice* is a key word. At first these maneuvers may seem difficult, especially if you have been quilting in another way. Keep at it; the more you quilt, the better your performance will be.

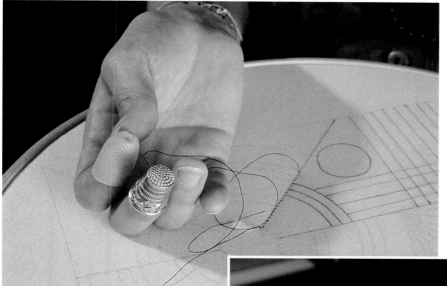

*Note*: Although I am a left-handed quilter, the photos that follow have been reversed so that the majority of quilters can follow them more easily. If you are left-handed, like me, use reversed hand positions.

To start a line of quilting, you can sink a knot into a seam allowance hidden inside the quilt or you can leave a tail of thread, which later will be woven into the line of stitching and anchored. See the final page of this chapter.

In the photo above, wearing a thimble and a fingertip cut from a yellow rubber glove, I have just drawn the thread through the quilt from my last stitch. The thread is running over the palm of my hand.

I grab the thread with my ring finger and pinky and tug on it just a little. This changes the angle of the needle and pulls the needle so that more of it is below my finger and thumb than above. I can also nudge the needle down even further with the side of my thimble, if necessary.

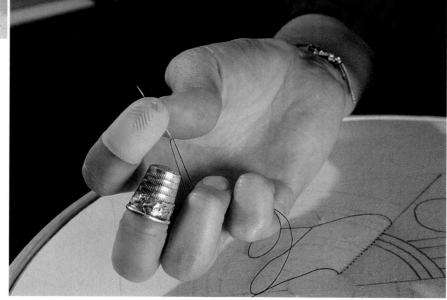

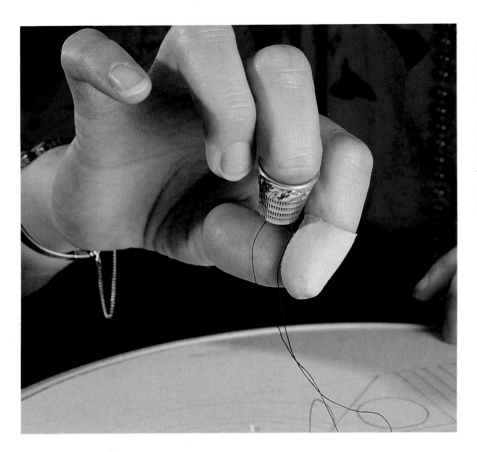

I then flip my hand over, pointing the vertical needle at the surface of the quilt, and park the eye of the needle in a dimple, or indentation, of the thimble.

At the same time, the middle or index finger of the off-hand (the hand beneath the quilt) has come to rest at the underneath surface of the quilt. The finger is not pushing against the underneath surface but just resting there.

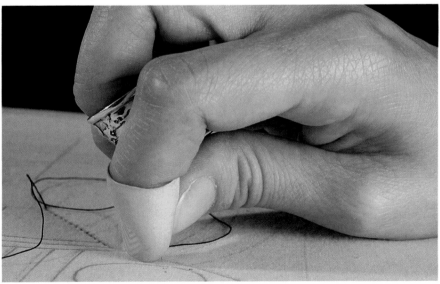

Then I set the point of the needle, which is straight up and down, on the surface of the quilt. (All but the tip of the needle is hidden here by my index finger.)

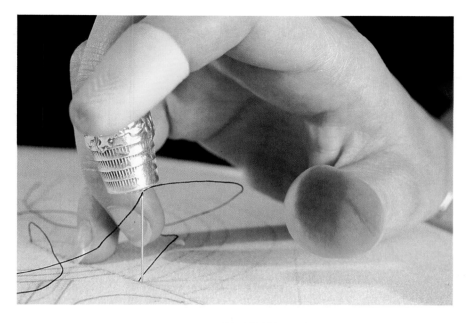

At this point, I release my grasp of the needle with my index finger and thumb. Only the thimble should be touching the needle, and it is not pushing the needle—just stabilizing it. Because the needle is pointed and because the fabric is porous, the needle can be set easily in the surface of the fabric. With no further pressure, it will probably pass down to the batting layer and stop. I am reminded at this point of gymnasts who, after a successful vault or tumble, land on both feet with their arms outstretched, as if to say, "Ta-dah!" So this step, in which the needle is set in the surface of the quilt vertically, balanced by the thimble and free from the index finger and thumb, is called the "Ta-dah." For quilters used to manipulating the needle with the index finger and thumb, this is a difficult position for the fingers to assume. The thimble is all-important and is doing all the work.

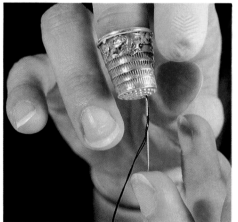

To practice stabilizing the needle with just the thimble, without pushing, try balancing the needle between the thimble and a finger of your left hand. This will teach you—in a hurry—not to push too hard!

After the Ta-dah, drop your thumb and rest it on the surface of the quilt. Your wrist also should rest on the surface of the quilt, not hover up in the air. (This will force you to use the small muscles of your fingers instead of your shoulder muscles as you continue quilting.) You should be able to hold this position for half an hour or longer—it should be that stable! You'll definitely want to hold the position long enough to check that your needle is entirely vertical before you continue.

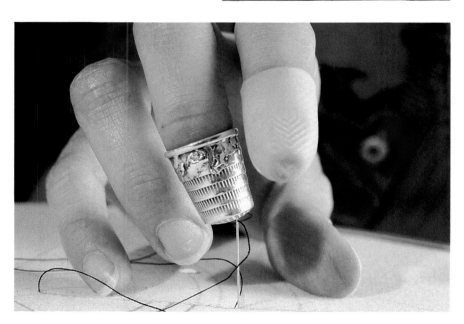

As the thimble stabilizes the needle in a vertical position above the quilt, either the middle finger or index finger of the hand beneath the quilt begins a gentle brushing movement on the underneath surface of the quilt, almost as if it's "looking" for the needle. When the needle exits the backing, it should lightly move over two, three, or four fingerprint ridges of your fingerpad. Why does the offhand finger engage in this brushing motion? Just think: When you enter a fabric store and spot a fabric that looks attractive, what do you do? You begin to stroke that fabric, saying, "Ahhh!" It's no fun at all to just touch or pinch the fabric—it's the stroking movement that heightens the sensation of touch. When the finger underneath the quilt is brushing the fabric, it will feel the needle exiting the backing more quickly, before the needle can prick the offhand finger.

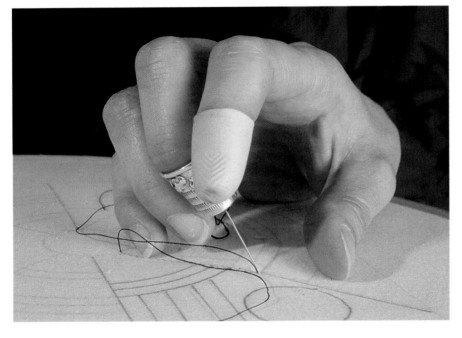

Once the off-hand finger has felt the tip of the needle exiting the quilt, let the thimble begin an arc downward that will bring the needle from a vertical position to a perfectly horizontal one. Notice that the thimble is at the same angle as the needle, as both move down toward a position horizontal to the surface of the quilt.

When about one-third of the arc has been completed, as in this photograph, it is safe for the finger on the off-hand to begin pushing up against the quilt. That finger is no longer in danger of pushing against the point of the needle; now it will be pushing against the side of the needle.

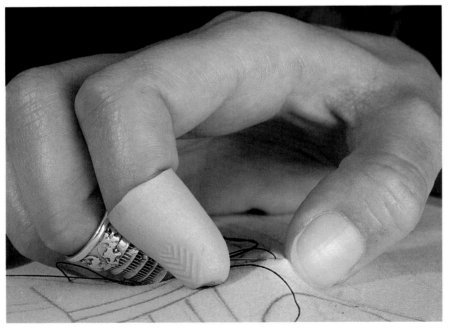

While the off-hand finger is pressing up, the thumb of the hand holding the needle is pressing down, just a little bit in front of the point of the needle; the two motions occur simultaneously to create a little hill of fabric and batting just in front of the needle. The harder you push—up from the bottom and down from the top—the smaller that hill will be and the smaller will be the stitch to come.

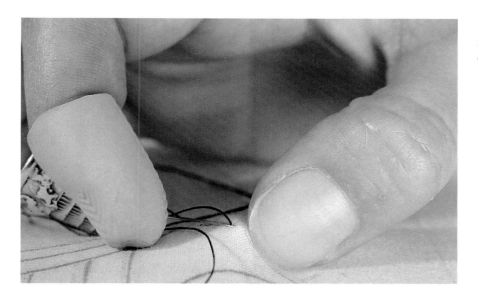

Finally, with the thimble, push the needle through the little hill until it exits.

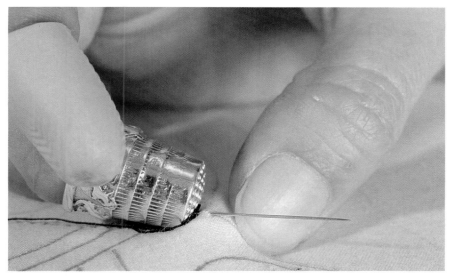

Push the needle all the way through.

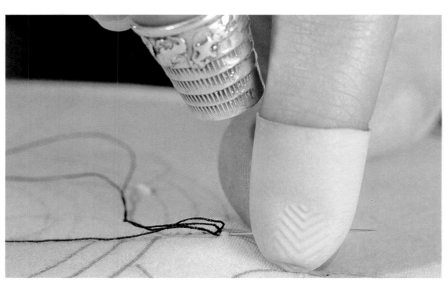

Then grasp the needle between your index finger and thumb and pull it through the quilt. (The fingertip cut from the rubber glove and worn on your index finger now comes into play, giving you greater traction.) Congratulations! You have completed a single stitch.

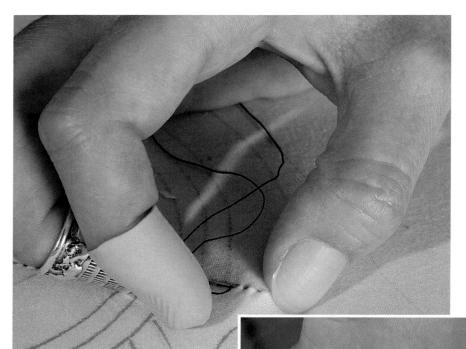

Practice making single stitches until you become comfortable with this approach and can perform the various steps in a flowing movement. This may take some time, especially if you are accustomed to handling your needle in another way. You may find that your stitches seem to become worse before they begin to improve. Don't worry—you'll get better.

Once you can make single stitches with ease, you can begin working on the more efficient "rocker" stitch, in which you load several stitches on your needle at once before pulling it through.

To perform the rocker stitch, follow the steps to make a single stitch just until the point of the needle emerges from the little hill. Then use your thimble to return the needle to the vertical position and make a second single stitch. Load as many stitches as you can make in about ¼ inch of the fabric onto the needle before you pull it through.

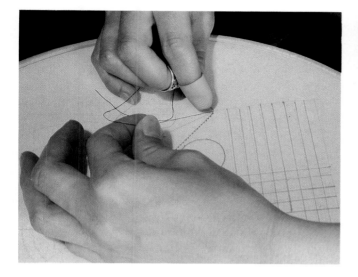

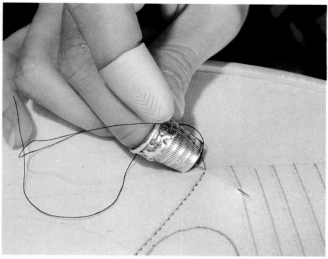

To end a line of quilting, you can bury your thread end in the batting by weaving the thread invisibly through the line of quilting you have just completed. Insert your needle into the hole that the thread has just exited. Now you are ready to weave.

To begin weaving, bring the point of the needle out of the quilt top at one side of the line of quilting. (See the photo above.)

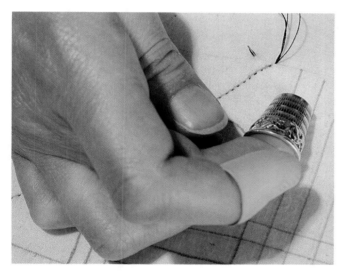

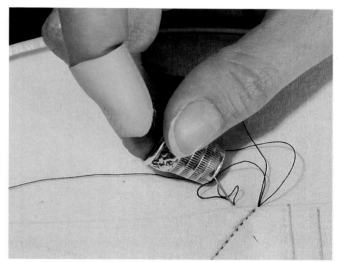

Grasp the needle by the pointed end and pull the needle until the eye of the needle has passed through the line of quilting inside the batting but has not come out of the quilt. Now, holding the needle by the pointed end, pivot the needle and push the eye back through the next-to-last stitch in the line of quilting and out through the surface of the quilt. (See the photo above.)

Then, holding the eye of the needle, pull the needle backwards until the point has passed through the line of quilting but has not yet come out of the quilt. Pivot the needle and push the pointed end through the second-to-last stitch in the line of quilting, and then out through the surface of the quilt.

Continue the process, weaving the thread back and forth through the line of quilting, until the thread end is securely anchored. Clip the thread end close to the fabric. Stroke the quilt lightly with your fingernail to remove any distortion in the quilted line that may have been caused by the weaving. (*Note:* If you began the line of quilting by leaving a tail of thread, you can also anchor that thread tail with the weaving process. First take 1 "fake" stitch—hitting the top and the batting but not the backing of the quilt—*backwards*. Then begin to weave, as shown above, in the direction you have just sewn.)

# A Quilter's Holiday

Combine a quilting workshop led by a favorite teacher with a week's vacation in a lovely setting—that's the winning formula for a quilter's holiday. For this special report, *Quilt with the Best* traveled to Scotland with noted quilter, writer, and quilt historian Helen Kelley, of Minneapolis, Minnesota.

For the many quilters around the world who have delighted in her speeches and for thousands more who follow "Loose Threads," her monthly column in *Quilter's Newsletter Magazine,* Helen Kelley's is an important voice in quilting. Her presentations are polished (the gift of background training in theater and radio) and lively, infused with her enormous personal warmth and energy. Beyond that, it's clear that her fascination with the history of quilts and other textiles is more than just an interest—it's a passion.

"I have a love affair with history," she says, "especially with the Renaissance, a period in which symbolism—in textiles and other arts—was widely used as a means of personal expression. Personal expression is my focus; I'm intrigued with the ways that textiles, throughout history and around the world, have been used to express cultural values and emotional truths."

Helen's own quilts, widely published and admired, are often contemporary reinterpretations of traditional quiltmaking styles. Her *Crazy Jubilee* uses crazy-quilt techniques to portray Queen Victoria. *Norwegian Elf* borrows design elements from Scandinavian rosemaling; *Mother Goose* is pieced from tiny squares in the technique known as postage stamp quilting. "I find

*Glory in the Morning,* 28" x 32½", 1991

making each quilt an adventure," Helen says, "and usually like to try a different type of quiltmaking—just to see if I can do it."

One traditional form of special interest to her is the American Indian needlework technique known as ribbonwork. Helen first became acquainted with this technique during a research visit to the University of Kansas.

Indian needleworkers of the Woodland tribes, as early as the 17th century, obtained silk ribbons from French traders. By layering the ribbons and cutting, turning back, and

---

*I'm intrigued with the ways that textiles, throughout history and around the world, have been used to express cultural values and emotional truths.*

---

stitching the upper layer in reverse appliqué, they made distinctive ribbon-strip designs with which to ornament their clothing. In time, the technique became highly developed and spread westward. Ribbonwork is still practiced today among Indian needleworkers, who use it to ornament dance clothing and other special garments.

Helen learned more about ribbonwork, through historical research and through attending powwows and other contemporary Indian festivities. Taking along her stitchery, she made friends with Indian needleworkers, whom she found unfailingly generous in sharing their love of and expertise in this traditional art. At length, ten years of research and design exploration culminated in the publication of her book *Scarlet Ribbons: An American Indian Technique for Today's Quilters* (American Quilter's Society, 1987).

In summer 1991, Helen made a teaching visit (her second) to Park House, a quilter's retreat in Scotland. "It's a magical place," she says. "Students come with holiday expectations, to explore new needlework techniques in an atmosphere of freedom and excitement." As a topic, she chose to present the native American technique of ribbonwork to her students from the British Isles. In a special Isle of Arran series of quilts (see page 49), she reinterpreted favorite British design motifs—thistle, shamrock, daffodil, and rose—in ribbonwork style. In *Glory in the Morning,* pictured on this page, she also created a companion piece to the Isle of Arran series, with American flowers and using printed fabrics, which yield a softer design effect.

# Quilting at Park House

In July 1991, *Quilt with the Best* followed Helen Kelley to Scotland to record a quilter's dream holiday at Park House, on the Isle of Arran. In this quiet country setting, sheep graze peacefully in green fields that stretch down to the sea, flowering shrubs tumble over stone walls, and foxglove and thistle line the winding roads.

Ken and Judy McAllister purchased Park House ten years ago and have been working since then, along with their son Grant, a talented woodworker, to bring the old farm back to life. The large white farmhouse now offers a warm welcome to guests from around the world, who enjoy the comfortable surroundings and the delights of Judy's kitchen (such as roast lamb with fresh mint sauce, garden-fresh peas and potatoes, or steaming bowls of carrot soup flavored with orange and coriander).

Just beyond the house, an old piggery—first converted to a popular tea room—has been remodeled into a quilters' studio. Each of the former stalls is now a student bay, fitted out with a handsome pine table and bench. Troughs have become flower beds, and skylights positioned among the heavy wooden beams admit a lovely light.

This unusual studio draws quilting students from across the British Isles and also from Denmark, Holland, Austria, France, Germany, and America. Each set of students soon becomes a congenial group, united by the common bond of quilting and the McAllisters' gracious Scottish hospitality. "Park House is a real quilter's retreat," Judy says. "It radiates lots of happiness and companionship."

From March to October, week-long quilting sessions (each limited to six students) are taught by visiting teachers, most of them British, or by Judy, who is herself an accomplished quilter and quilt teacher. Past topics have included miniature quilts, crazy patchwork, rotary cutting techniques, freezer paper appliqué, charm quilts, and curved Log Cabin patchwork.

Classes meet each weekday morning; during the afternoons, quilters can return to the studio to continue their work or use the time to enjoy this beautiful island. Drives along the more than 50 miles of coastline road offer spectacular views of the sea. Each of the dozen or so villages along this main road has its own special character; most have intriguing shops—including craft shops—to explore. Hiking and pony trekking lead to scenes of great beauty and often geologic or archaeological interest. With natural gifts that include more than 40 species of birds, 45 species of ferns, and a huge variety of wildflowers, Arran is a wonderful place for bird-watching, beachcombing, and photography. Golfing, fishing, and hill climbing are also activities that many visitors enjoy.

*Ken and Judy McAllister welcome visitors to Park House, a quilter's retreat on the Isle of Arran.*

*As Helen and two students examine a ribbonwork dress and shawl, a gust of wind through the garden turns the pieces into bright banners.*

*Even in July, Arran's mild climate can bring cool days. A woodstove in the Piggery keeps things cozy as the quilters work.*

At breaks, the group gathers for cups of tea and treats like Judy's sweet and buttery shortbread.

What's a quilting class without a bit of a quilt show? Outside the Piggery, Helen displays her quilt Magic, as students' cameras click away. (Also see page 45.)

In a week-long quilter's retreat, there's plenty of time for individual instruction and small-group discussion.

The companionship of fellow quilters, an inspired teacher, a new technique to learn. . .

. . .and quiet time to stitch. It's a quilter's holiday dream come true.

If you would like more information on quilting holidays at Park House, send your name, address, and $1 to cover postage and handling to:
Judy McAllister
Park House
Corriecravie
Isle of Arran, Scotland
KA27 8PD

The Isle of Arran lies off the west coast of Scotland. In the summer months, ferries move back and forth throughout the day, bringing holiday travelers drawn by the island's great natural beauty. Hiking, climbing, pony trekking, and enjoying the many species of birds and wildflowers are popular pastimes.

## AND THOU BESIDE ME

*And Thou Beside Me* is Helen's interpretation of the very old quilting technique *broderie perse*, in which precious bits of printed fabric were cut apart and appliquéd to a whole-cloth background to form a new design. In Helen's quilt, design elements from six or more contemporary chintz fabrics were arranged and appliquéd around a traditional tree trunk shape to form a graceful new picture. The piece is shown on a garden wall at Park House.

*And Thou Beside Me*
32" x 40"
1982

*From the more than 50 miles of coastline
road that circle the perimeter of the island,
superb views of the sea abound.*

*Summer on Arran is filled with flowers, whether wildflowers like these shown nestling among one of the many native species of ferns (above), or these bright blossoms (at left) from the castle gardens at Brodick.*

*Beachcombing is a fascinating pursuit along these shores. Because of the island's complex geological history, many interesting types of stones can be found. In places there are exquisite shells; and here and there, you may find mysterious jewels that prove, at closer look, to be man-made—bits of crockery and green glass worn smooth by the waves.*

## MAGIC

The large quilt *Magic* (shown also on page 41) stretches the concept of ribbonwork. Moving away from simpler patterns of symmetry, the ribbons here diverge in a spectrum of colors. Ribbon appliqué spans the ribbonwork and fills in the background of the piece.

*Magic*
59½" x 82"
1989

*Turnings, 22" x 45", 1986*

## TURNINGS

*Turnings*—like the quilt *Magic,* a personal expression in ribbonwork—illustrates still other ways in which the technique can be expanded. Here, ribbonwork is cut into patchwork shapes and resewn. The various ways in which the leaf design is turned show a further expansion of the basic design idea.

This quilt appears, with full instructions, in *Scarlet Ribbons: An American Indian Technique for Today's Quilters* (American Quilter's Society, 1987).

*Arran offers many sites of great archaeological interest, like this, one of the Bronze Age standing stones, a short hike from the main road on Machrie Moor.*

*A highlight of a tour of Arran is a stroll through the gardens of Brodick Castle. Originally the seat of the Dukes of Hamilton, the castle (portions of which date from the 14th century) and its 600-acre estate are now owned by the National Trust of Scotland and are open to the public. Displayed within is a fine collection of silver and porcelain.*

## Unicorn Quilt

Made in celebration of a grandchild's birth, Helen's *Unicorn Quilt* is a contemporary interpretation of Renaissance *mille-fleurs* tapestry.

The quilt is stitched with appliqué on a pieced background and is a translation of the Lady-and-Unicorn tapestries in the collection of the Cluny Museum in Paris. As in those historic tapestries, the plant and animal images in this quilt symbolize various virtues and ideals.

*Unicorn Quilt,* 46" x 60", 1987

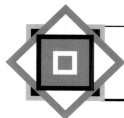

# Helen Kelley's Ribbonwork Garden

The flowers in American Indian ribbonwork design are created with strip appliqué. For 200 years, Indian women have made beautiful lengths of silken flowers to trim their clothing by layering ribbons, cutting a design hole in the top ribbon, and reverse-appliquéing it to the one beneath. The colored ribbon underneath then actually becomes the flower.

Indian women slowly and patiently marked and needle-turned their appliqué from silk ribbons. It was a slippery, tenuous, time-consuming technique. Instead, we will make our "ribbons" from 100-percent-cotton fabric strips, which will crease well and handle easily.

To begin, you must choose your pattern. I have created 3 patterns—beginner, intermediate, and advanced—for each of the 4 featured flowers (shamrock, rose, thistle, and daffodil), so that you can choose the level of challenge you wish.

Beginner patterns feature a large, single flower with edges that are easy to shape. These patterns offer beginners in appliqué a good introduction to the ribbonwork technique.

Intermediate patterns require you to make 2 somewhat smaller flowers; the lines are still fairly simple. The pair of flowers in each intermediate design form a mirror image, a design formula frequently used by Indian ribbonworkers.

Advanced patterns are for needleworkers who are experienced in appliqué. The advanced designs are repeated along a full length of "ribbon" (that is, a fabric strip cut across an entire width of fabric) to make a total of 4 flowers. These 4 flowers can then be cut apart into patchwork shapes and resewn in interesting configurations. The advanced designs are of the size and complexity of Indian ribbonworkers' flowers.

The 3 pieces of my Isle of Arran quilt series, shown here, give an idea of designs that can be made with beginner, intermediate, and advanced blocks. Decide the level at which you would like to work and turn the page for details on how to make the templates required. You'll need tagboard (a white cardboard), paper, carbon paper, and a pencil.

**Advanced**

**Beginner**

*Isle of Arran I,* 25" x 25", 1991

**Intermediate**

*Isle of Arran II,* 29" x 29", 1991

*Isle of Arran III,* 31" x 37", 1991

# Beginner Templates

## Beginner Shamrock

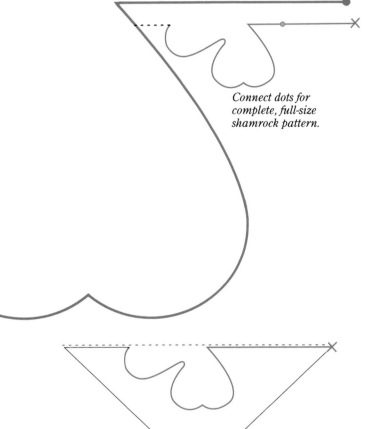

Stem

*Connect dots for complete, full-size shamrock pattern.*

The following pages offer 4 floral designs, each of which will make lovely ribbonwork. In our instructions, we'll focus on the shamrock design, for 2 reasons. First, its gentle curves make it an easy pattern to work with. And second, my name just happens to be Kelley!

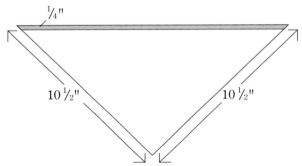

¼"

10 ½"       10 ½"

To make a beginner template, cut a 10½-inch right triangle from tagboard. Mark a line ¼ inch inside the long edge of the triangle (shaded in the diagram above) and trim away the shaded area.

Trace the shamrock pattern shown above onto a piece of paper, connecting the dots for a full-size pattern. Then, placing the X on the pattern at the right-hand corner of the triangle as shown, transfer the pattern to the template triangle, using carbon paper. (You need not trace the portion of the design—the stem—that runs along the edge of the template.) Trace over the carbon paper lightly because you don't want carbon paper lines to transfer to your fabric later on.

Using paper scissors (small, sharp scissors with curved blades work best), trim out the shamrock motif. Make sure that the cuts are neat, leaving no sharp points or flat edges on your cutout shape. (Points on your templates will make a pointy fabric shape.) Label one side of the tagboard template with an "A." Turn the template over and mark the other side "B."

In the same way, you can make beginner templates from the other beginner patterns on pages 52-53.

# Intermediate Templates

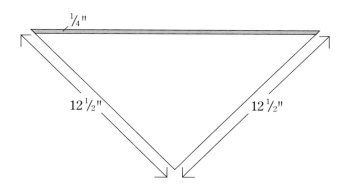
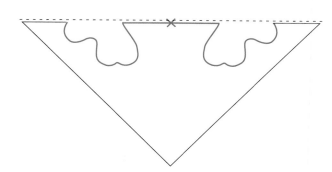

To make an intermediate template, cut a 12½-inch right triangle from tagboard. Mark a line ¼ inch inside the long edge of the triangle (shaded in the diagram above) and trim away the shaded area. Mark the center point of the long edge with an X.

Trace an intermediate shamrock pattern (see page 55) onto a piece of paper. Place the X of the pattern on the center point marked on the long edge of the triangle and transfer the pattern line to the tagboard template with carbon paper, tracing lightly. (You need not trace the portion of the pattern—the stem—that runs along the edge of the template.) Turn the paper pattern over, reversing the design, and trace the pattern again onto the template, as shown. Trim away marked shapes with paper scissors, leaving smooth, neat curves. Label one side of the template "A" and the other side "B."

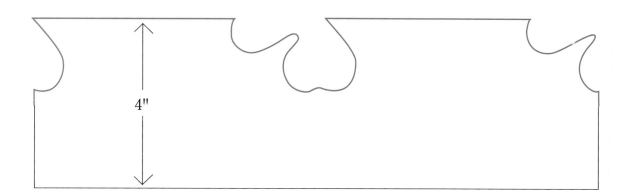

## Advanced Templates

To make an advanced template, cut a 4-inch by 15-inch strip of tagboard. Trace an advanced shamrock pattern (see pages 54-55) onto the paper, connecting the dots for the complete design. Tracing lightly over the carbon paper, transfer the design to one edge of the strip. (You need not trace the straight line between the shamrocks that runs along the edge of the template.) Note and trace the partial-design repeat elements at either end of the strip. With paper scissors, trim away any excess strip length. Trim away the shamrock design, leaving smooth, neat curves. Label one side of the template strip "A" and the other side "B."

# Additional Patterns

*Connect the dots for complete, full-size patterns.*

## Beginner Rose

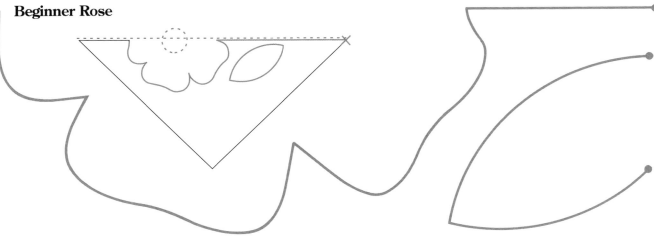

## Beginner Daffodil

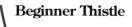
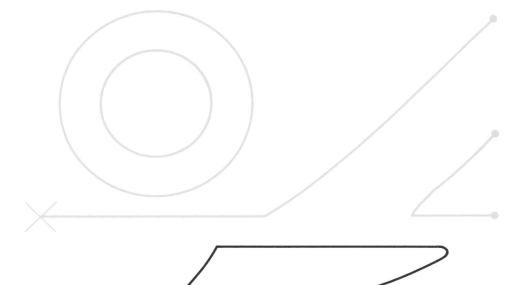

## Beginner Thistle

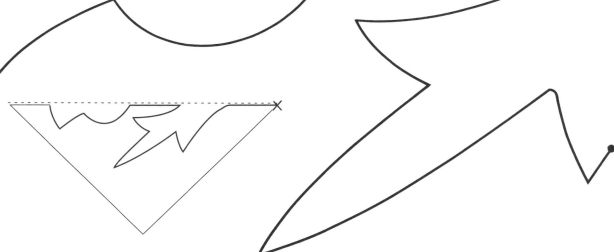

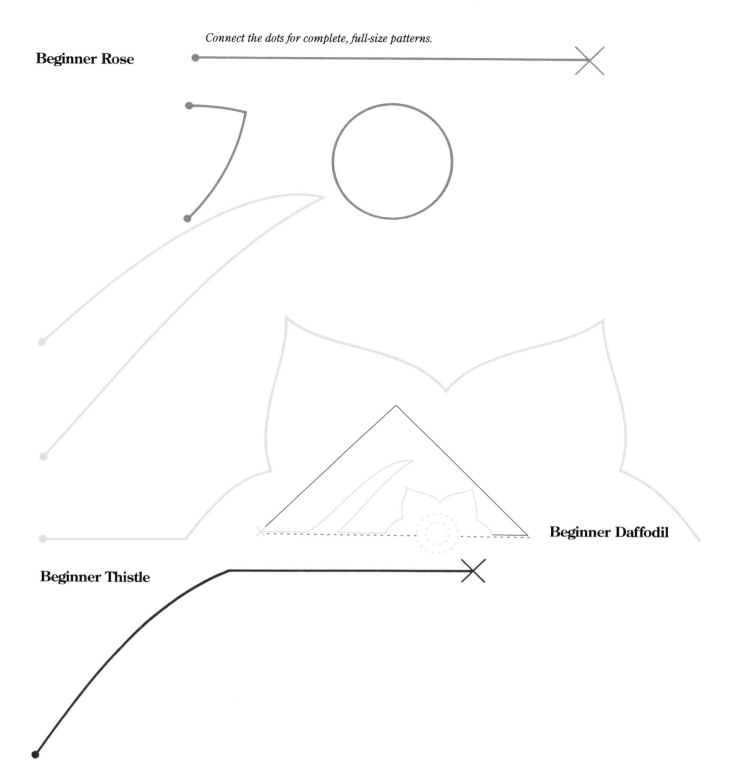

*Connect the dots for complete, full-size patterns.*

**Beginner Rose**

**Beginner Thistle**

**Beginner Daffodil**

# Additional Patterns

**Intermediate Rose**

**Intermediate Daffodil**

**Advanced Rose**

**Advanced Daffodil**

**Advanced Thistle**

**Advanced Shamrock**

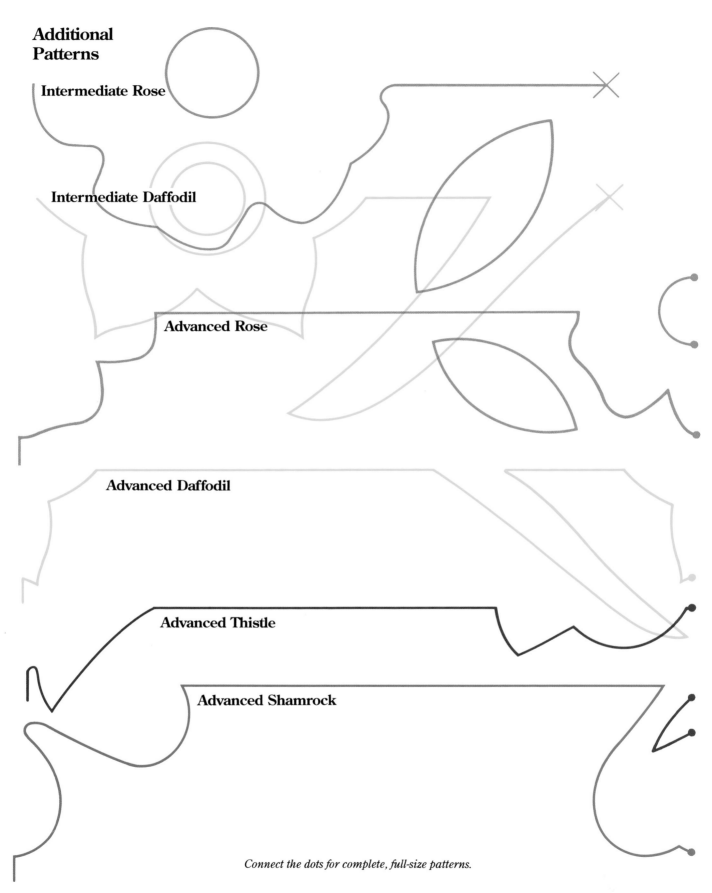

*Connect the dots for complete, full-size patterns.*

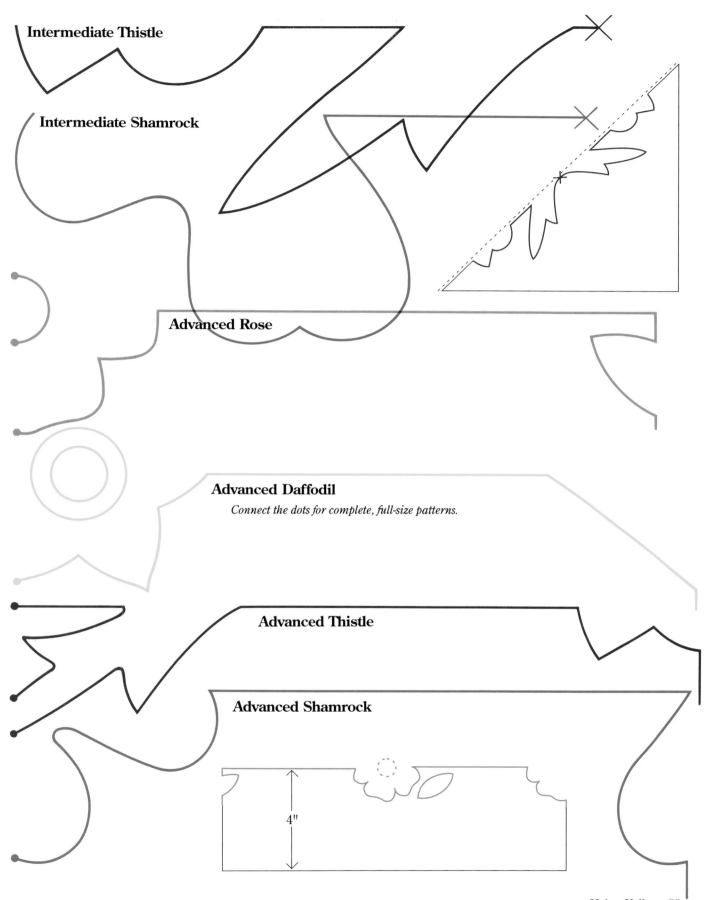

**Intermediate Thistle**

**Intermediate Shamrock**

**Advanced Rose**

**Advanced Daffodil**

*Connect the dots for complete, full-size patterns.*

**Advanced Thistle**

**Advanced Shamrock**

4"

### The Beginner Block

To make the beginner shamrock block, you'll need:

A piece of tagboard at least 10½ inches square

4 pieces of 100-percent-cotton fabric: ½ yard each of 2 background colors and of 2 shades of green for the shamrock. Keep in mind that these need not match in exact shades or tints of the same color. Actually, a bit of clashing of colors is much more exciting. Yellow-green and blue-green together are lively and interesting.

Thread to match fabrics

A sewing machine (if none is available, you can seam pieces by hand)

An ironing board and iron

Spray starch

A protector cloth

A basic sewing kit, including sharp sewing scissors and fine needles

With your rotary cutter, cut 1 (9-inch by 18-inch) "ribbon" from each of your 4 fabrics. (*Note:* For future reference, remember that ribbon strips are most stable and easiest to handle when they are cut lengthwise on the fabric. However, for this project, in the interest of economy, we will work with our ribbons cut across the width of the material.)

Join the 2 pieces of green (shamrock) fabric, stitching with a ¼-inch seam along 1 long edge of the pieces. These seamed strips will be the base for your ribbonwork. Press the strips open from the right side, ironing into the seam line to remove any tucks and folds, and opening the strips completely.

Now let's get down to the fun of serious business. Before using the spray-starch appliqué technique, cover your ironing board with a protective cloth. (This can be something as simple as an old piece of sheet from your rag box.) I have never had any damage to my appliqué fabric, but the build-up of starch on the ironing board can turn it into a gummy mess. The ironing board needs to be fairly firm. If you have one of those soft, springy sponge pads on your board, remove it. Then you're all set.

Place your first piece of background fabric on your ironing board, wrong side up. (Remember, since we are working in reverse appliqué, a hole must be cut into the background fabric so that it will reveal the green shamrock fabric that will later be placed beneath it.) On top of the fabric strip, position your tagboard template, "A" side up, so that ¼ inch of fabric can be turned back over the top edge of the template. Stab 2 or 3 pins through the tagboard and into the ironing board to secure the template, as in the photo below. (Those lovely sharp pins with the bright-colored plastic heads are not a good idea for this project; if your iron touches them, the heads will melt into creative blobs.)

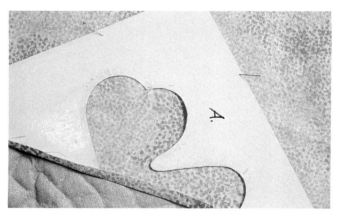

Now, using your scissors, carefully cut away the fabric that is exposed in the pattern holes of the template,

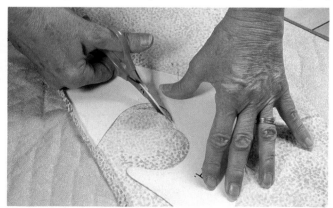

leaving ¼ inch of the fabric for seam allowance. (See last photo on page 56.) Clip into the seam allowance where the fabric forms an inner curve, freeing the seam allowance fabric to fold back over the template in a smooth curve when you shape it. You'll find the work easier to handle if you cut and shape the design in portions rather than cutting one large hole in the beginning.

With the fabric cut away, you are ready to shape the appliqué using the spray-starch method. Now, hear this! This is a learned technique. You will be awkward at first, but you will get better with practice. Eventually you will shape perfect appliqué with ease. Empty any water from your iron, because steam scalds fingers and you will be ironing close to your fingers. You cannot, however, burn your fingernails. I do, in fact, let the nail on my left forefinger grow. It is not very fashionable, but it's a great tool.

Spray some starch from the can into the lid to collect some of the liquid. (Eventually, you will be able to spray starch directly on the fabric, but, in the beginning, you are apt to over-spray and create a slippery mess, a soggy template, and, perhaps, a scorched film on the sole plate of your iron.) Dip your finger into the liquid starch in the lid and dab it on the straight edge of the template, on each side of the cutout design. (I have seen all sorts of creative tools that quilters have used for dabbing starch on their templates or the exposed seam allowances of their fabric, but I still find that my fingertip works best for me. I always have it right where I need it.)

Using the tip and edge of the iron as a metal finger, turn the seam allowance back over the edge of the template in a straight, smooth line. The starch will steam a bit. Watch your fingers! Hold the iron in place until the fabric is dry. By ironing the straight edge into shape first, you will secure it, and this will help hold the template in place as you shape the rest of the design. Continue around the design, dabbing starch on the seam allowance and shaping it back over the template. The fabric may very well adhere to the template; if it does, the shaping will actually be easier to handle.

To shape the fabric around narrow curves, stroke the fabric into place and hold it with your fingernail while you iron it. Remember, again, that you cannot burn your fingernail.

Continue until you have shaped the seam allowance all around the entire cutout shape.

Then remove the fabric and template from the ironing board and hold them up to the light so that you can view them clearly to discover any folds and points you may have ironed in by mistake. You can deal with some of these by touching them up with your iron. Others can be turned in with your needle as you are applying the piece.

The long narrow projection in the shamrock shape will be a challenge that you can shape by working in tiny pleats, easing in the seam allowance. If you bend or damage the template while you are working, simply dab on some starch and press the tagboard back into shape.

Use the point of a needle or seam ripper to loosen the fabric from the tagboard. Then, in one smooth motion, pull the fabric away from the template. (See photo below.) Carefully touch up any of the edges that were ruffled in the process of removing the template.

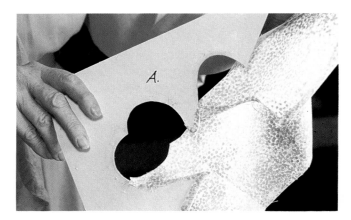

Lay the cutout strip on the top of one of the green base strips, with the shamrock color showing through the shaped hole. Pin the cutout strip in place, leaving a ¼-inch space between the turned-under edge of the top fabric and the seam line of the 2 green fabrics. This exposed channel of green is called "piping." Appliqué the cutout strip in place using matching thread.

Go back to the ironing board and lay out the second piece of background fabric to make another cutout strip. Turn the template over to the "B" side and arrange it on the fabric.

Shape it in the same way. Remove the template and pin the shaped fabric along the opposite side of the seam line on your shamrock-colored base so that the design is completed. Again, leave a ¼-inch channel exposed, this time showing the second green fabric. Position the points of the design opposite each other. Sew the second shaped piece in place.

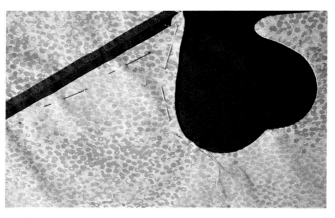

Turn your ribbonwork over and carefully trim away the excess green fabric from behind the background fabric, leaving neat edges. If you have used tiny appliqué stitches, you can trim as close as ⅛ inch. This will make quilting easier later on.

Take your strip to the cutting board. You are about to say a prayer, take a deep breath, and cut your piece into a geometric shape that you can use for patchwork. For the beginner block, make a 10½-inch-square tagboard template. Mark a diagonal line across the center of the template, to be positioned on the central seam line of the ribbonwork strip. Place the template on top of the ribbonwork piece. (See photo just below. In this instance, Arran "A" indicates the beginner block.) Mark around the edges of the template with a chalk pencil (or with what is my favorite marker, a soap sliver). Remove the template and cut along the marked lines to obtain a block ready to use in patchwork. (See second photo below.)

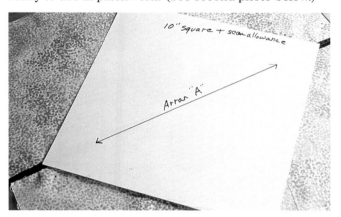

Make additional blocks, using the other beginner flower designs, if desired. Then you will have the pleasure of experimenting in placing them together to form the basis of a patchwork piece. (See the photo in the upper right-hand column.) Paper squares with light/dark value divisions may be used as a design model to suggest various ways of arranging the blocks. When you have decided on the arrangement you like best, seam the blocks together and add a simple border.

This is the formula I used for piecing *Isle of Arran I* (below). I quilted the blocks in this piece with echo quilting, working out from each design, and finished with a simple quilting design in the border.

*Isle of Arran I*

## The Intermediate Block

To make the intermediate block, first read through the instructions for the beginner block to get an overview of the basic process. Although the design elements in the intermediate block are somewhat smaller and more difficult to appliqué than those of the beginner block, the overall procedure is much the same. Here are a few important differences to note:

For the intermediate block, you will need a square of tagboard at least 12½ inches square; that is the size of the template for the intermediate block. When cutting your fabrics, cut 1 (10-inch by 20-inch) piece from each of the 4 fabrics.

After you have completed the intermediate ribbonwork strip, mark the 12½-inch-square template with a central diagonal line, just as for the beginner block, and cut out blocks so that the design is centered in each block.

In *Isle of Arran II* (above, at right), I simply joined 4 intermediate blocks together, as in the beginner piece. Intermediate quilters may wish to add a more elaborate set of borders. Repeated floral motifs, marked with the appliqué templates, are used in quilting these blocks.

*Isle of Arran II*

## The Advanced Block

To make the advanced block, first read through the instructions for the beginner block for an overview of the process. For the advanced block, cut 1 (4-inch by the width of the fabric) piece from each of your 4 fabrics.

When you have completed the shaping process for the first floral motif and have removed the tagboard template from the fabric strip, reposition the template by placing the partial-motif repeat on the end of the template into the already-shaped design. (See the photo below.) This will give you the proper template position for shaping your second floral motif. Continue working down the first fabric strip until you have shaped 4 repeats of the same design.

Appliqué the first background strip in place; then shape and appliqué the second strip. (See photo below.)

To cut out the pieces for the advanced block, you will need a different kind of template. Cut out a triangular template based on diagonally halving a 9½-inch square (this includes seam allowances). Mark a placement line 3¼ inches up from the base of the triangle and cut out a shamrock shape showing proper placement of the motif within the template. Lay your triangular template with the base toward you and the placement line along the central seam line. Mark it on the fabric. Then flip the triangle template around so that the apex is toward you and mark again. Mark 4 triangles across the width of the ribbonwork.

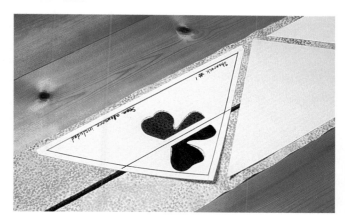

When you have cut the strip into 4 triangles, you can experiment with placement. (See photo in upper right-hand column.) Be careful with any of the cut patchwork pieces, since you have cut across hand-sewn seams and created some vulnerable bias edges. When the pieces are finally sewn into patchwork blocks, they will be stable and reliable.

You will discover that you have made some delightful flower shapes, but, even better, you have created repeated patterns that will echo in intriguing shapes when they are arranged. The light and dark geometric shapes can be used to form backgrounds of pinwheels, streaks of lightning, and such.

If you have trimmed your ribbonwork neatly, quilting it should be an easy and exciting event. Again, the tagboard templates used in shaping the appliqué make excellent quilting design stencils. See *Isle of Arran III* (below). Note that in this advanced piece, additional ribbonwork strips are used in the borders.

*Isle of Arran III*

# MERIKAY WALDVOGEL:

# A Collector's Clues for Dating Quilts

Merikay Waldvogel purchased her first quilt in 1973. Just out of graduate school and armed with a master's degree in linguistics, she was about to embark on a career of teaching English as a second language to Chicago's immigrant children. While she was furnishing her new apartment, the eccentric quilt pictured at right caught her eye, and she was transformed, all at once, into a quilt enthusiast. Over the next several years, she continued to collect quilts—in Illinois, Wisconsin, Missouri—quilts like Log Cabin and Ocean Waves. She liked the old, traditional patterns, stitched up in strong, dark colors. But it was not so much the historical value of the quilts that mattered to her—their worth as textile records of the past—but simply their visual and tactile appeal.

In 1977, Merikay left Chicago for Tennessee and marriage to fellow Missourian Jerry Ledbetter. As progam director at the Knoxville Women's Center, Merikay found ways to bring her love of old quilts into her new life. She decorated the walls of her offices with favorites from her collection, invited noted quilt historians, like Chattanooga's Bets Ramsey, to present programs, and instituted an annual quilt show and seminar. Over time, Merikay's interest in quilts became well known in the area. People with old quilts to sell would call her, and her collection increased. Many quilts came complete with family histories and reminiscences. Merikay began to see her quilts not only as striking visual pieces, but as the records of lives. It became increasingly important to her to learn as much as she could about the history of each piece she acquired.

In 1982, officials of the World's

*Through quilts, I can learn American history, which never meant much to me before. I can learn women's history— untold women's history— and help to preserve that history.*

Fair to be held in Knoxville asked Merikay to organize a quilt exhibition for the Folklife Building. In pulling together this show, she widened her quilt horizons, meeting other collectors and growing familiar with types of quilts she had not seen in the Midwest.

Then, in 1983, Merikay began a major quilt adventure. She and Bets Ramsey, inspired by the Kentucky State Quilt Survey—an early development in the state quilt survey effort (which has grown, at this writing, to projects in 40 states and the District of Columbia)—decided to document quilts made in Tennessee prior to 1930. Working with an enthusiastic group of volunteers including state extension agents and quilt guild members, Merikay and Bets organized a two-year search for the historic quilts of Tennessee. Quilt Days were held in twenty-two locations—including schools, churches, and senior citizens' centers—and 1,425 quilts were documented.

As expected, the Quilt Days brought forth a full range of quilts, from rough, utilitarian works to elaborate appliquéd and stuffed showpieces. Some owners knew little about the history of their pieces. Others offered a wealth of information, including one family whose invitation to "come out to the house and see" led to an exploration of a treasure trove of 19th-century textile materials, family letters, and diaries. (This experience led to Merikay's special interest in linsey quilts and her research paper "Southern Linsey Quilts of the 19th Century," presented to the 1987 meeting of the American Quilt Study Group.)

The wealth of quilts seen at Quilt Days presented Merikay with an unusual opportunity to survey the evolution of American quiltmaking. "That was when things suddenly began to make sense in terms of dating quilts," she says. "When I saw hundreds and hundreds of quilts, they began to fall into categories." In 1986, a traveling exhibit of thirty representative quilts, chosen from the many seen at Quilt Days, began to tour, and a companion book, *The Quilts of Tennessee: Images of Domestic Life Prior to 1930,* was published.

In 1988, Merikay was asked by the Knoxville Museum of Art to be the curator of another traveling quilt exhibit. The theme selected was "Depression Era Quiltmaking." Since quilts from the Depression Era have often been undervalued by collectors and historians, Merikay took it as a challenge to unearth the little-known details of the story. She interviewed quiltmakers, consulted magazines and newspapers of the 1930s, and chose thirty quilts to tell the story. For Merikay, the central question in this area of research became "How can these quilts look so pretty when they were made in such hard times?" In 1990, the exhibit opened and her accompanying book, *Soft Covers for Hard Times: Quiltmaking and the Great Depression,* was published by Rutledge Hill Press.

New research projects—some of them growing out of her work with thirties quilts—currently intrigue Merikay. And she continues to do research on her own quilt collection, which has grown to around 80. Of these quilts, she especially treasures the unusual ones and those whose makers are known. Several of her quilts have appeared in exhibits, books, and magazines.

Recently, she has served as consultant to the developers of a hospital and a shopping mall. Both groups plan to install quilt collections in their facilities.

And though Merikay continues to teach English as a second language, her work with quilts increasingly fills her time. In addition to her writing, Merikay lectures to quilt groups, historical societies, and groups of school children. "Dating Quilts" and "Quilt Photography" are her most-requested workshops.

For Merikay, the networking, the striking of common chords involved in quilt study, has become a way of life. "My interest in quilts," she says, "is everything for me. Through quilts, I can learn American history, which never meant much to me before. I can learn women's history—untold women's history—and I can help to preserve that history. And it's a way of meeting people, an intergenerational thing. I really like talking with older people and getting their stories." For this avid collector, quilts now offer far more than an exciting visual experience—they offer insight, a livelier way of looking at the past that Merikay delights in sharing.

*Members of the Thursday Bee, many of them volunteers in the Tennessee State Quilt Survey, examine a quilt for clues to its date.*

# Dating Quilts with Merikay Waldvogel

Many people think dating quilts is a mysterious process involving a secret code only given to a chosen few. In fact, it is a fascinating pastime that even a beginner can enjoy after learning a few simple guidelines. As with most new skills, your ability to date quilts will improve quickly with practice.

As a quiltmaker, you already have a wealth of information to use in dating quilts. You know the process, the terminology, and the materials of quiltmaking. What has changed over time are the styles, choice of fabrics, and tools, as this nation evolved into the industrialized society we live in today. By looking for evidence of changes in these areas, you can date your antique quilts.

In pages to come, we'll review some major shifts in American quiltmaking styles, set in a time line of historical events, including developments in the textile industry that directly affected the availability of quiltmaking resources. Read the captions carefully. Notice how styles alternate between formal and informal. By looking at style changes over time, you can get an idea of the eras in which certain types of quilts were most often made.

We'll also move in closer for a detailed look at a few quilts, to look for additional clues in their colors, fabrics, and construction details. Again, read the captions and examine the photographs of quilt details carefully. Look around in your community for other quilts to compare to these examples. By analyzing a number of quilts, you will develop your own set of reference quilts to keep in mind. For example, I often refer to a tattered Album quilt (dated 1873) that I bought years ago (you'll see a photograph of it on page 70). Whenever I see similar solid green fabric or brown prints, I feel quite certain that the quilt in question was made in the 1870s.

But a word of caution is in order: Dating quilts is anything but an exact science! Dating a quilt by style or pattern alone is dangerous, because there have been frequent revivals of earlier styles throughout American

history. Think of the current quilt revival. Quiltmakers of the 1990s are experimenting with many early styles—cutout chintz, crazy quilts, string quilts, and others.

Dating a quilt by its fabric alone may also lead to errors; we quiltmakers know that quiltmakers are ardent fabric savers! Today's quilts often include fabric saved by others or fabrics from quilt tops collected at garage sales and antique stores.

We also know that quilt projects can be put aside and picked up again years, maybe even generations, after they were started. Even dates inscribed on quilts should be confirmed by other evidence in the quilt, for a date may or may not represent the date the quilt was completed. It may, in fact, signify the birth, marriage, or anniversary of the maker or the receiver.

What we must do is estimate the date of a quilt based on a number of different clues and then make a final estimate based on the latest possible date. Quilt-dating authorities sometimes split their estimates by making statements about both the fabric and the finished quilt. For example, they may say, "The fabrics appear to be pre-Civil War; however, the fan quilting would indicate a post-Civil War date."

With these goals and ground rules in mind, turn the page. First, test your knowledge of quilt history by trying to guess the relative ages of four quilts from the historic Ramsey House in Knoxville. Then let's learn by looking at a variety of interesting antique quilts and quilt details.

# Exploring Quilt History

**Get a "feel" for the history of quilts** by familiarizing yourself with as many examples of historical quilts as you can. Read quilt books and magazines. Attend quilt shows; browse through galleries and antique shops. And don't overlook the historical homes and museums in your area.

With Merikay Waldvogel, we visited the Ramsey House on Thorngrove Pike in Knoxville, once home to Colonel Francis Alexander Ramsey, who was prominent in Tennessee history. Costumed docents welcomed us to this National Historic Site, which is being preserved and restored by the Association for the Preservation of Tennessee Antiquities.

**Test your knowledge of quilt history** by ranking four quilts from the Ramsey House collection (shown on the following page) in order of age. Which is the oldest? (See answers below.)

---

Answers: C, B, A, D

C. Compass Variation (pre-1850). This pattern, probably the quiltmaker's own invention, is typical of the earliest pieced patterns based on simple geometric shapes. The fabrics, dyed brown, indigo, and green, are early roller prints. The backing is made of a coarsely woven white cotton cloth. The quilting is intricate—typical of early 1800s quilts, rather than late 1800s quilts. See "Early Pieced Quilts," page 68.

B. Tulip Appliqué (1850-1860). This pattern, too, is probably the quiltmaker's own invention. She has formed four wreaths of flowers, using fabrics in the popular color combination of the mid-1800s—pink, red, green, and yellow—and framed them with a delightful winding vine. The quilting is very intricate. The binding has an inset cording. See "Appliqué Quilts," page 69.

A. Pickle Dish (1880-1890). Though this pattern looks like the 20th-century Double Wedding Ring and its condition might make a beginning dater of quilts think it was the newest of the four quilts, this quilt dates from the 19th century. The pattern of this piece is called Pickle Dish, and the beige fabric was probably once a dark teal blue green often found in late 19th-century quilts. It is difficult to date quilts made with solid fabrics, but this green fading to beige is a very strong clue. The green fabric, probably dyed with a Prussian blue mineral dye, has faded to a buff color. See "Pieced Quilt Pattern Explosion" and "Post-Civil War Solid Fabrics," on page 70.

D. Whole-Cloth quilt (1920-1940). Whole-cloth quilts with a center medallion design quilted into the surface were among the earliest quilts made in America. They often included elaborate stuffing and stipple quilting. The style had died out by the time of the Civil War. However, quilts like this reversible whole-cloth quilt were introduced in the 1920s and 1930s and marketed as "boudoir" quilts. Decorators revived a very old quilt style and created a bedspread that complemented the Early American furnishings of the modern urban woman. See "Boudoir Quilts," page 73.

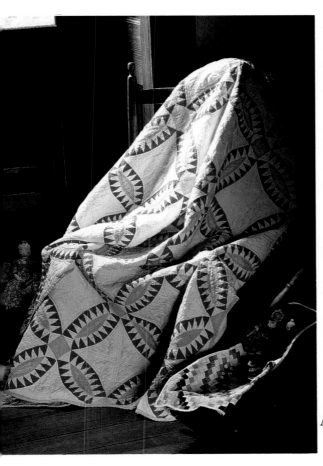

Center medallion quilt, South Carolina, 1820, private collection

Star quilt, Tennessee, 1820, collection of Ruth DeFriese

### CENTER MEDALLION QUILTS (1790-1840)

Quilts with a central focus, popular until the 1840s, seem to be a carryover from British traditions. Quilts made in many parts of the British Empire continued this center medallion style. American quiltmakers, however, broke with this tradition about 1840 and began to make quilts pieced from equal-sized blocks, a design innovation still important in the American quilt tradition. Whole-cloth quilts (made of one solid-colored top) continued to have elaborate quilting with a central focus.

**1790** Cotton gin invented by Eli Whitney; spinning is soon powered by steam engine, invented by James Watt.

### EARLY PIECED QUILTS (1820-1870)

The earliest pieced quilts were simple combinations of triangles, diamonds, and squares. The Star pattern was an early favorite. As this red-and-white star quilt (made around 1820) demonstrates, simple shapes, repeated, could be elaborated into intricate and exciting designs.

Other favorite pieced patterns of the early 19th century included Variable Star, Album, Mariner's Compass, Double X, Basket, and Feathered Star.

**1830** Roller-printed multicolored fabric available. (Prior to this, fabric had been printed using copper plates or—still earlier—with wooden blocks.)

**1846** Sewing machine patented by Elias Howe.

Center medallion quilt, South Carolina, 1820, private collection

**CUTOUT CHINTZ** (1790-1850). Motifs were actually cut out of a piece of chintz, rearranged, and appliquéd to a white cloth. The chintz fabric was imported from England and France and appears most often in areas near seaports, such as New England, Virginia, and South Carolina.

The Cross quilt, New York, 1850, collection of author

**ROLLER-PRINTED FABRIC** (1840-1870) appeared in the U.S. by the 1800s. The cloth was run through roller presses two or more times to apply different colors. Proper registration (or the lining up of colors and figures) was sometimes difficult. The earliest fabrics have thick lines around figures to hide mistakes.

Mosaic, New Jersey, 1860s, collection of author

Appliqué, Greene County, Tennessee, 1850s, collection of Namuni Hale Young

## ENGLISH TEMPLATE-PIECED QUILTS (MID-1800S)

English template piecing involves cutting out numerous paper templates (often hexagons, diamonds, or squares) and pieces of cloth (often silk) which are slightly larger than the paper templates. A cloth piece is wrapped around and basted to each paper template; then the pieces are joined with tiny whipstitches. Although this technique remained popular in Britain, Americans preferred the running stitch for quiltmaking, and English template piecing became less common in America.

## APPLIQUÉ QUILTS (1850-1890)

Rather than follow the cutout chintz appliqué tradition, American quiltmakers began to create their own appliqué motifs cut out of solid cloth (often red, pink, green, and yellow). Popular patterns, which included Rose of Sharon, Princess Feather, and Whig Rose, were passed on and duplicated or adapted. The height of this appliqué style occurred prior to the Civil War, but some women renewed their interest in this type of quiltmaking after the war ended.

**1800s** Expansion into American West.

### Dating Guidelines:
Quilts made before 1850

Machine quilting: None

Edges: Straight

Binding: Usually—separate, straight-grain binding applied over edges of quilt.

Quilting: Typically—close lines of tiny stitches. Often—complex motifs. Occasional stippling and stuffing.

SOLID COTTON FABRICS (post-1840). The green fabric shown here is called chrome green and was produced by overdyeing indigo blue with a chrome yellow dye. The other dyes used in making the fabric shown here are indigo, chrome yellow, and Turkey red, all of which were colorfast.

Appliqué quilt, Greene County, Tennessee, 1850s, collection of Namuni Hale Young

54-40 or Fight, Ohio, 1880s, collection of author

Sampler, New England, 1880s, collection of Linda Claussen

## LINSEY QUILTS (1865-1890)

During the Civil War, Southern women revived home weaving traditions in order to provide bedding and warm clothing for their families and soldiers. Linsey is a heavy, scratchy cloth made of a cotton warp and a wool weft on a simple loom. Only solid, striped, or checked fabrics were possible. Following the war, this cloth was incorporated into utility quilts. Since the quilts were thick and bulky, the quilting designs were usually simple and made with large stitches.

## PIECED QUILT PATTERN EXPLOSION (1880-1910)

Following the Civil War, entrepreneurs sought out untapped markets. Through mail-order magazines, businesses could reach millions of consumers. Many magazines featured quilt patterns, often contributed by their readers. Other readers could write in to order the patterns by name and number or could simply copy the patterns for themselves. This sampler quilt is made of patterns featured in magazines published in the 1880s and 1890s.

**1861-1865** Civil War.

**Late 1800s** Communication and transportation systems, such as postal service, roads, and railroads, are expanded. Continued movement west.

**1870** Textile mills return to the production of cloth for the home. A calico explosion results. Prints are varied. Browns, dark blue, and reds predominate.

**1870** The sewing machine is promoted and sold widely.

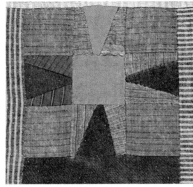

54-40 or Fight, Ohio, 1880s, collection of author

LINSEY QUILTS (1865-1890). Since linsey is made of a cotton warp and a wool weft, look for the white specks that indicate the cotton warp threads. The fabric is coarse, thick, and ravels easily. Other fabrics in this quilt are all cotton. The navy cloth was called jeans.

Album quilt, Knox County, Tennessee, 1873, collection of author

POST-CIVIL WAR SOLID FABRICS AND BROWN PRINTS (post-1865). The solid green fabric, dyed with Prussian blue mineral dye, fades easily to a pale beige. The earlier chrome green will not fade so drastically. The detailed brown prints are also an indication of a post-1865 quilt.

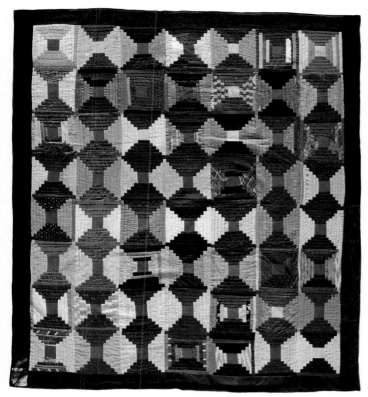

Log Cabin: Courthouse Steps variation, Pennsylvania, 1880s, collection of author

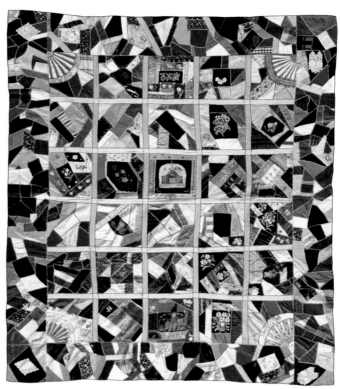

Crazy quilt, Massachusetts, 1890, collection of author

## LOG CABIN QUILTS (1870s-1890s)

This quilt shows the variety of fine wool fabrics available after the Civil War. Log Cabin quilts were a popular way to use sewing scraps to create visually exciting quilts. A small square (usually red or yellow) was sewn to the center of a square of foundation cloth; strips were then sewn to each side of the square in sequence. Log Cabin quilts made on a foundation are usually tacked or tied rather than quilted. Log Cabin quilts not made on a foundation are usually later quilts.

## CRAZY QUILTS (1880-1920)

At the U.S. Centennial Exposition in Philadelphia in 1876, demonstrations of British embroidery and art work from Japan enthralled American needleworkers. Both influences combined in a new quilt style—the crazy quilt, a fad until the 1920s. Odd-shaped pieces of cloth (often silks, satins, and velvets) were basted to a foundation, and the raw edges were covered with decorative embroidery stitches. Embellishments included embroidered flowers, animals, stars, and sequins and ribbons.

**1865-1890** Increased trade with Asia: Japanese and British influences are evident in home furnishings and therefore in quilts. Elaborate crazy quilts with lots of embroidery in motifs of flowers, fans, birds, animals, and spider webs are common.

**1880-1901** Victorian Period.

---

**Dating Guidelines:**
Quilts made in the late 1800s

Machine stitching: Often seen in binding, sometimes seen in appliqué.

Edges: Straight

Binding: Usually—separate, straight-grain binding applied over edges of quilt. Sometimes backing is brought forward over quilt top and stitched down (or vice versa) to finish quilt.

Quilting: Widely spaced stitches in designs simpler than those seen in pre-1850s quilts. Favorite simple designs include fan, parallel lines, cross-hatching, and outline.

Caesar's Crown, 1880,
collection of The Mall at Johnson City (Tennessee)

CHROME ORANGE (1870-1890). This shade of orange appears in quilts as late as the 1930s; however, it is more common in quilts in the late 19th century. Here chrome orange appears along with another popular 19th-century color, Turkey red.

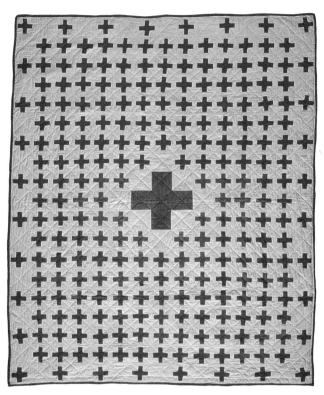

Red Cross fund-raising quilt, Tennessee, 1918,
collection of Rose Center and Council for the Arts, Morristown, Tennessee

String top, East Tennessee, 1920s , collection of author

## FUND-RAISING QUILTS (1920s)

As early as the mid-1800s, quilts were used as fund-raisers. Quilts were raffled, or money was given and the donors' names inscribed on the quilt. This quilt, made to benefit the Red Cross, was modeled after a design in *Modern Priscilla* magazine, December 1917. Its maker used an ingenious, time-saving method of inscribing the names, simply typing them on the muslin squares with the red half of her typewriter ribbon.

## STRING QUILTS (1900-1950)

The string-piecing technique, like crazy quilt and Log Cabin, requires a foundation for each block. However, the foundation in string quilts is often paper rather than cloth. When the blocks are joined together, the paper is removed before quilting. Newspaper scraps left on the back of unfinished string quilt tops contain information that aids in dating the fabrics. String quilts remained popular through the Great Depression and World War II, when fabric was scarce.

**1917-1918** U.S. fights World War I.

**Early 1900s** U.S textile industry flourishes, but the quality of the product decreases. Also, U. S. textile companies begin to invent their own dyes, which previously had to be bought from Germany. Fabrics are brightly colored and cheap.

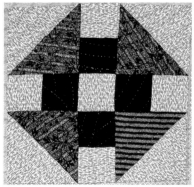

Churn Dash, Georgia, 1890, collection of author

MOURNING PRINTS (1890-1920). The fabric appears to be a black fabric with detailed white figures printed on it; in fact, it is white fabric with black print. These dress prints show up often in late 19th-century quilts.

Charm quilt top, Loudon County, Tennessee, 1890,
collection of Rachel Huff Wilson

OTHER COTTON PRINTS (1890-1910). Intricate, colorfast prints that feature sporting designs, paisleys, stripes, and other figures appeared in red, blue, maroon, and brown in the late 1800s.

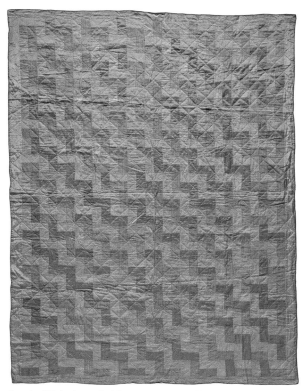

Streak of Lightning quilt, Minnesota, 1920s, collection of author

## BOUDOIR QUILTS (1920s)

As America entered the 20th century, traditional quiltmaking lost popularity in the urban areas. Quilt patterns appeared less widely in women's magazines. However, in the 1920s, decorative boudoir quilts, stitched in pastels, achieved a short-lived popularity. This one is a traditional pieced Streak of Lightning. Other, more common, boudoir quilts are whole-cloth, reversible quilts with quilting around a center medallion. (See quilt D on page 67).

*Oriental Poppy* ( made from a Marie Webster pattern), Tennessee, 1930, collection of Sandy Kilgore

### REVIVAL OF
## CENTER MEDALLION QUILTS (1912-1940)

In 1911 and 1912, the *Ladies' Home Journal* published Marie Webster's quilts. Her quilts, tailored to fit the bed and made with colors that harmonized with the decorating style of the time, established a new direction in quilting and created new interest in quiltmaking. First sold by mail-order from Marion, Indiana, her patterns eventually were adapted and sold by Stearns & Foster on the wrappers of Mountain Mist batting.

**1920** Women gain right to vote.

**1920s** Good economic times.

**1929** Economic depression begins.

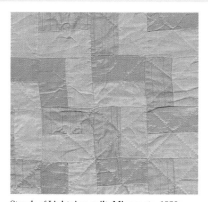

Streak of Lightning quilt, Minnesota, 1920s, collection of author

RAYON (1920s). In the 1920s, quilts might be made of the new, non-traditional fabrics, like the rayon of this piece.

---

**Dating Guidelines:**
Quilts made from 1910 to 1930

Machine stitching: Usually used in joining blocks and for binding.

Edges: Curved and scalloped edges appear, due to the introduction of commerical bias binding.

Binding: Bias binding appears, but traditional methods of finishing edges continue (see late 1800s, page 71).

Quilting: Intricate quilting designs return, as fancy quilts are re-introduced as part of the Colonial revival style in home furnishings.

---

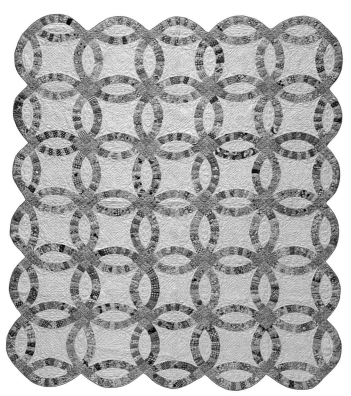

Double Wedding Ring, Tennessee, 1930s, collection of Michele MacDonald

*Dogwood*, Tennessee, 1930s, collection of Jeane Hilliard

### POPULAR PIECED PATTERNS (1920-1950)

Near the end of the fast-paced 1920s, Americans yearned for simpler times and renewed their interest in quiltmaking. Hundreds of patterns were available (many through local newspapers). As economic conditions worsened, women filled their time with stitching. Thousands of quilts were made with patterns such as Double Wedding Ring, Grandmother's Flower Garden, Dresden Plate, and Sunbonnet Sue. Most were made with pastel figured cloth.

### DOGWOOD APPLIQUÉ (1930-1950)

This quilt, made from a pattern offered by Stearns & Foster, has the center medallion construction popular in quilts from the early 1800s. However, the difference in age is obvious. Appliqué flowers from the 20th century are usually realistic representations of the flowers they portray. Also, the gray-green fabric used in this quilt is a far different shade from the yellow-green fabric that was commonly used in the 19th century.

**1930s** The Great Depression.

**1933** Sears National Quilt Contest at Chicago World's Fair.

**1933** President Roosevelt's recovery programs begin.

Double Wedding Ring, Tennessee, 1930s,
collection of Michele MacDonald

PASTEL PRINTS (1920-1940). The palette of colors changed radically in the 1920s. The pastel colors predominated. Fabrics were available in a wide range of lively geometric designs.

*Dogwood*, Tennessee, 1930s
Collection of Jeane Hilliard

SOLID FABRICS (1920-1940). During this period, the hues of solid fabrics softened. Apple green, lemon yellow, eggshell blue, and orchid were favorite colors, used often in quilts.

*French Wreath* (made from an Anne Orr pattern), Michigan, 1930s, collection of Beth Dyer

## PROFESSIONALLY DESIGNED PATTERNS (1930-1950)

Anne Orr was among the professional quilt designers who drew inspiration from the early center medallion quilt style. In this pattern, offered by *Good Housekeeping,* Orr, who was a prolific needlework designer, used small squares, pieced together to look like the cross-stitch patterns for which she was best known.

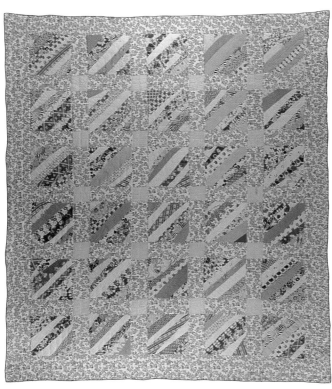

String quilt, Tennessee, 1940, collection of Dot Davis

## FEED- AND FLOUR-SACK STRING QUILTS (1930-1950)

Utilitarian quilts such as this one were most common during the Great Depression and World War II. This quilt was made of patterned feed-sack cloth, put together with a string-piecing technique. White fabric from feed sacks had been used in quilts since the late 1800s; figured cloth sacks began to appear about 1930.

**1940s** Textile industry turns its attention to the war effort. The small amount of cloth that is produced for home use is mainly for children. The motifs are large and depict children at play, animals, and cowboys and Indians.

**1941-1945** U.S. fights World War II.

**1950s** Modernization of U.S. Modern appliances for the homemaker are promoted. Traditional needlework is discouraged as "old-fashioned."

---

### Dating Guidelines:
#### Quilts made from 1930-1950s

Machine stitching: Sometimes used in piecing and in binding. Rarely used in appliqué.

Edges: Straight or scalloped

Binding: Usually bias binding is employed, but traditional methods of finishing edges continue (see late 1800s, on page 71).

Quilting: In utility quilts, parallel lines, fan, and outline quilting continue. Commercial quilt patterns, such as feather circle, feather border, and spider web appear in the plain blocks of fancier quilts.

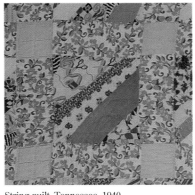

String quilt, Tennessee, 1940, collection of Dot Davis

FEED- AND FLOUR-SACK CLOTH (1930-1950). This sack cloth was printed to look like store-bought cloth. Look for the small line of holes left from the stitching of the flour or feed sack to be sure you have a quilt made of sack cloth.

# QUILT HISTORY AND DOCUMENTATION

Quilt owner's name _____

City_____State_____Zip_____

Telephone (home)_____(work)_____

What relation, if any, to the quiltmaker?_____

Is there a story connected to this quilt?_____If so, record: _____

_____

_____

_____

Owner's name for quilt (if any):_____

## History of quilt, according to owner:

Place made:_____
       City       County      State

Date made:_____

Quiltmaker:_____

Born_____/_____/_____at_____

Died_____/_____/_____at_____

Parents_____

Spouse_____

Children_____

If quilt is signed or dated, quote and describe.

_____

_____

Where inscribed?_____

## Awards quilt has received and/or published references:

_____

_____

_____

Quilt reviewed by:_____

# Recording Your Family's Quilt History

As a student of quilt history, one of the first things you'll want to do is to record the history of your own family quilts and others that you may own. Use the form on the page opposite to document as much as is known about the quilts in your collection.

I also encourage you to attach quilt information to the back of each quilt. As the photograph shows, I put a piece of muslin into my typewriter and type all the information I know, as well as my estimate of the quilt's date. Then I loosely baste this piece of muslin to a corner of the quilt's backing. Incidentally, since I typed this label, I have done further research on linsey quilts. The date made should be circa 1870.

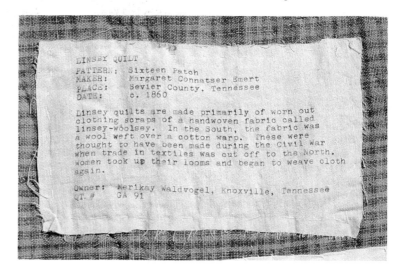

# Expanding Your Quilt Knowledge

I hope this brief review of quilt history may be the beginning of a satisfying new hobby for you. Seek out opportunities to practice your new skill—continue to look at quilts in publications, antique stores, and museums. Before reading the captions and labels presented with quilts, try to make your own estimates of each quilt's age. If you disagree with the date assigned by the owner or exhibitor, ask yourself why. Consult other quilt authorities. You may find that your estimate is more accurate. Quilts appear in many places: I like to estimate the age of quilts appearing in movies to see how well the quilt matches the era depicted in the film!

Some of you will want to take the next step in quilt research, which is publishing your findings. One day you may come upon a group of quilts or a particularly interesting quiltmaker. Authenticate the quilts, confirm the facts given to you, and write a paper or book. You will need to compare your findings with traditional historical references, such as textile histories, travel accounts, genealogical records, journals, and diaries. Don't be afraid to contact quilt experts. Ask them to read your paper and make comments and suggestions. You will be embarking on a journey of wonderful discoveries.

To discuss the possibility of publishing your findings, or simply to join with other quilt enthusiasts in the enjoyment of quilts past and present, you may wish to contact the American Quilt Study Group, 660 Mission Street, Suite 400, San Francisco, CA 94105, (415-495-0163). This national nonprofit group, which is devoted to uncovering

and recording the ongoing history of quiltmaking, is made up of members from across the nation and from nine foreign countries. Its annual seminar is held each October. The research papers presented there are published in an annual review titled *Uncoverings*.

As I have studied quilts, I have developed a better understanding of American history. I have tapped into a national network of people with similar interests, and I have come into contact with women whose life stories would never have reached the traditional history textbooks. I hope you gain as much satisfaction from this new interest as I have. Please don't hesitate to contact me for advice and suggestions. (See the faculty listing on the final page of the book.)

## Suggestions for Further Reading:

Brackman, Barbara. *Clues in the Calico: A Guide to Identifying and Dating Antique Quilts.* McLean, VA: EPM, 1989.

Brackman, Barbara. *Dating Antique Quilts: 200 Years of Style, Pattern, and Techniques.* San Francisco: American Quilt Study Group, 1990.

Liles, J. N. *The Art and Craft of Natural Dyeing: Traditional Recipes for Modern Use.* Knoxville: University of Tennessee Press, 1990.

Montgomery, Florence. *Textiles in America 1650-1900.* New York: Norton, 1984.

# Reach for the Unexpected

"I don't know if teaching is genetic," says Margaret J. Miller of Woodinville, Washington, "but I do come from a long line of teachers. My great-grandfather was a teacher in a one-room schoolhouse in Minnesota. My grandmother was a home economist. My father was a college professor, and his sister was a home economist who taught in community colleges for years. It's something I grew up with."

And whether it's nature or nurture, there is no doubt that Margaret Miller's innovative approaches to quilt design—and her ability to encourage creative work in her own students—are stirring up quilters across the nation and as far away as Australia.

"I think of teaching as a performance—getting people excited about something. First, *you* have to be excited yourself, and, when the topic is quilting, that's easy for me. Then you can present your students with a spark, a precious nugget of an idea—an insight—and encourage them to see what they, in turn, can do with it. What's fascinated me about taking classes from quilters whose work I've admired is this: They present a design problem to the group, and the learning comes not so much from what they say as from watching all the other students solve the problem. That's the atmosphere I try to create in my classes—an atmosphere in which people feel free to explore and realize that they're

*Bloomin' IV*, detail

*What's fascinated me about taking classes from quilters whose work I've admired is this: They present a design problem, and the learning comes not so much from what they say as from watching all the other students solve the problem. That's the atmosphere I try to create in my classes—an atmosphere in which people feel free to explore and realize that they're bound to discover something no one else will.*

bound to discover something no one else will." And for Margaret, exciting directions to explore in quilting seem limitless. In her "Bloomin' Quilt Grids" workshop, a portion of which is presented in this chapter, students learn how to manipulate the grid underlying traditional patchwork blocks to create a wide range of exciting new effects. In "Strips that Sizzle," another popular workshop, she suggests ways to enliven traditional strip-piecing techniques for new impact. And in a brand new class, "Round Pegs in a Square Hole," she explores setting wedge-shaped blocks in curvilinear paths that beckon quilters into whole new territories of quilt design.

Margaret's boundless creative energy has been expressed in a life-long love of needlework of many types, a love that was fostered by her Scottish mother, also an avid needleworker. But finding a career in which that love could lead the way has required a search with several twists and turns.

"You know, when you're a bright student, people are always asking you what you plan to study in college. When I was a girl, one of the 'approved' answers to that question was 'nursing'; I found myself replying often that I planned to become a nurse, and I got lots of approval for that. Gradually I became convinced that a career in nursing lay ahead for me. I got right up to the point of filling out my application for the University of Maryland. I just had to fill in the computer dot indicating that I wanted to attend the School of Nursing and—to my surprise—my pencil would *not* touch the page! I was amazed, because I thought it was all settled."

After some thought, Margaret opted instead for a course of study in home economics, with a major in clothing and textiles. She went on to earn a master's degree in home economics from the University of Wisconsin.

Later, married and with two sons, Margaret had her first real teaching opportunity at California Polytechnic State University in San Luis Obispo. Among other courses, she taught a class in creative textiles that drew on all her needlework skills and required her to learn still others. At this time, she learned quilting and appliqué techniques so that she could share them with her students. As a class, they toured needlework businesses in San Francisco and Los Angeles.

Intrigued by what she had learned about the needlework business and increasingly drawn to quilt design, Margaret began her own business, Tanglethread Junction. She sold appliqué patterns nationwide at quilt stores and quilt shows. After several years, however, Margaret realized that her real interest lay in innovative design and teaching rather than in developing and selling patterns.

She gives much of the credit for this change of direction to Nancy Crow, with whom she studied in 1981. Nancy Crow's praise of her work during that class seemed to Margaret to come both as encouragement and admonishment: "That workshop with Nancy Crow changed my life. She was the first one who seemed to say to me, '*You* have a special talent, and *you* have to do something with it.'"

During the ten years that have passed since the realization that quiltmaking was to become the focus of her creative energies, Margaret has built a teaching schedule that keeps her traveling throughout the year, sharing her ideas on quilt design across the country and abroad. In the spring of 1991, her first book, *Blockbuster Quilts* (Bothell, WA: That Patchwork Place) offered quilters everywhere a treasure trove of innovative approaches to designing with traditional patchwork blocks.

And the work goes on. "I've come to understand that I have a special gift," Margaret says, "like a special coal glowing inside me that I must guard at all costs. That's why I was put on this earth—to make my quilts. Not a day goes by that I don't treasure that gift; I am so privileged to have found something that I really want to do."

Margaret Miller often identifies her quilts with specially designed, hand-stitched labels, like this one sewn to the backing of her quilt *Sea Route*.

# Margaret J. Miller's "Bloomin' Quilt Grids"

This design system, "Bloomin' Quilt Grids," began as I was doodling traditional quilt blocks on graph paper, looking for ways to make those blocks "sing a new song." An element that many blocks, especially 4-patch and 9-patch patterns, have in common is the use of only 2 angles, a 90-degree angle and a 45-degree angle. It occurred to me that one way to breathe new design life into these traditional blocks would be to incorporate some other angles in addition to or instead of just those 2 angles.

When you change the outer perimeter of a traditional block—from a square to a rectangle, for example—many of the angles within the block change automatically. Horizontal and vertical lines do not change angles, but any diagonal lines do change. (See Diagram 1.)

With these changes, the pieced

design suddenly seems to have curved lines without requiring any curved seams. This, then, is the magic of the system "Bloomin' Quilt Grids": Changing the angles yields the illusion of curved lines or even of a dome shape arising in the middle of the quilt. (This latter variation led to the naming of the design approach; the blocks seemed to "bloom" in the center of the quilt, as in my *Bloomin' IV*.)

This workshop is an introduction to "Bloomin' Grids" line and design as well as color strategies for these and other pieced surfaces. The color strategies are explored through the making of mockups or

puzzles made of real fabric pieces. (Before they are cut into puzzle pieces, the fabrics are glued to index cards for stability. Then, even if the design work is done in miniature, the fabric pieces will have sufficient body to be handled with ease.)

Quilts developed with this design system certainly cannot be made in a single evening or with very few templates. However, they will be treasured for their unique design quality over the years, and numerous distinctive quilts can be derived from a single set of templates. The visual complexity of quilts from "Bloomin' Grids" is such that many different color strategies can be applied successfully to the same graphic surface. Thus, a quiltmaker can really test the many design possibilites of a given design by working in a series. My quilts *Bloomin' IV* and *Bloomin' V*, for example, were both made from the same templates, yet they look very unlike each other because of the different use of color in the 2 pieces.

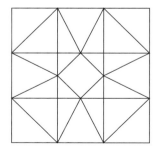

**Diagram 1**

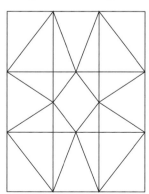

*Bloomin' IV*
79" x 79"
1986

This quilt shows most markedly the illusion that the blocks "bloom" or expand in the center of the quilt, as though the quilt were laid on a spherical, rather than a flat, surface.

*Bloomin' V*
79" x 79"
1987

This quilt is made from exactly the same pattern as *Bloomin' IV*. The same templates can produce numerous and varied quilts, depending on how color is sprinkled across the pieced surface.

### Things You Will Need

Pencils (mechanical, with 0.5-mm lead, or #2 lead pencils with a pencil sharpener)

Eraser

Rulers: 2-inch by 18-inch and 1-inch by 6-inch (Do not use Plexiglas straightedges for rulers; they cast a shadow on the graph paper.)

Graph paper: 11-inch by 17-inch pad of "cross section" graph paper, 8 squares to the inch

Tracing paper: 1 roll, or same-size (or larger) pad as graph paper

Colored pencils

Scissors for paper

Rubber cement and glue stick

Posterboard: 1 (22-inch by 28-inch) white sheet

Rotary cutting equipment: Plexiglas straightedge; mat (cutting surface), large-wheel rotary cutter with old blade in it (for cutting index cards and fabric)

Reducing glass (or binoculars)

Index cards (5-inch by 8-inch), white (1 or 2 packages)

Spray adhesive

You will also need your favorite book of traditional patchwork patterns, especially 4-patch and 9-patch designs. Jinny Beyer's *Quilter's Album of Blocks and Borders* is a good one. Obtain access to a photocopy machine that can copy 11-inch by 17-inch sheets of paper and reduce designs. And you'll need a vertical design surface. It is easier to evaluate design and color from a distance and on a vertical surface rather than a horizontal one. For this workshop we will be working only with small (20-inch to 25-inch-square) posterboard mockups, which can be taped, pinned, or even propped up against a wall. But for creating full-size quilts you are encouraged to use 1 or 2 (4-foot by 8-foot) soundboard panels covered with flannel fabric. With these, you can cut a fabric piece and press it to the wall to evaluate it; you don't need pins. If the fabric piece works, fine; if not, take it down, cut another, and press it in place.) If your home does not allow for such panels, substitute a length of Pellon fleece suspended from a wall.

### Fabrics

Use as many different colors and values of fabric in this workshop as you can. You will be mounting swatches of your fabrics onto index cards. Your stack of cards ideally should include 1 card for each fabric you have in your collection— and then some!

Be sure to use light, medium, and dark fabrics. You should have a minimum of 24 different fabrics: at least 6 lights, 6 darks, and the rest in light-medium, medium, and dark-medium values. If your mind boggles at too many choices to make, restrict yourself to only 3 or 4 color families. For example, red-purples and teals, with some yellow-oranges and a few yellow-greens for accent, are 4 color families spread around the color wheel. You could also choose 3 color families that lie close together on the color wheel, such as red, purple, and blue.

Once you have your fabrics prepared, look them over to be sure that you have light, medium and dark values. You should have large, medium, and small prints, as well as solid fabrics.

For the mockup, you will be cutting very small pieces of fabric that will be glued to a piece of posterboard to make a fabric puzzle. These pieces will be easier to cut and handle if they are first adhered to a stable backing.

Therefore, cut swatches from all the fabrics you wish to use in the workshop. Cut your swatches slightly larger than the 5-inch by 8-inch index cards. Fabric swatches should be smooth and unwrinkled. Lay a number of index cards side by side outdoors on a patio or picnic table. Spray all the cards with spray adhesive. Press fabric swatches, wrong side down, to the cards.

### Procedure

The "Bloomin' Grids" system for designing pieced surfaces is based on a basic grid that is composed of 9-unit blocks. Some of these units are squares and some are rectangles. This basic grid is then rotated a number of ways to create the overall quilt design. The first step is to create the basic grid. We will go through the process with a 9-patch block called Doris's Delight, so that you get the feel of the design system.

### The Basic Grid: 9-Patch Patterns

Place 1 sheet of 11-inch by 17-inch graph paper horizontally in front of you on a table. In altering a traditional block, it is important to first draft the block in its traditional form; this helps you to understand the makeup of the block, and the draft serves as a reference during the block transformation process.

In the upper left-hand corner of the graph paper sheet, draw a square that is 12 graph paper squares on each side. (Do not work at the actual edge of the graph paper. Leave a margin of ½ inch or so.) Subdivide this square into thirds as you would in order to draft a 9-patch block into it. Each patch of this 9-patch block has 4 graph paper squares on a side.

Draft the block Doris's Delight into this 9-patch block. (See Diagrams 2 and 3.)

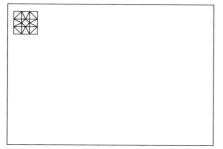

**Diagram 2**

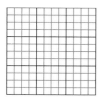 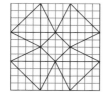

**Diagram 3**

The graph paper is called "cross section" because there is a heavier blue line printed every inch across the paper. On the first available heavy blue line to the right of the block you have just drafted, draw vertical line A. On the first available heavy blue line down from the top of the paper, beginning at line A, draw horizontal line B. (See Diagram 4).

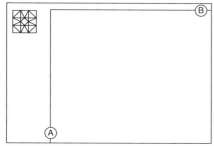

**Diagram 4**

Count 12 graph paper squares to the right of line A and draw a second vertical line (C) beginning at line B. (See Diagram 5.) *Note: From this point on, the lines may or may not fall on a heavy blue line on the graph paper.*

Count 18 graph paper squares to the right of line C and draw vertical D. Count 24 graph paper squares to the right of line D. Draw vertical

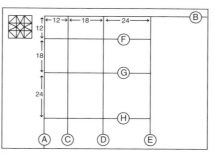

**Diagram 5**

line E. Count 12 squares down from line B and draw horizontal line F from line A to line E. Count 18 squares down from line F and draw horizontal line G. Count 24 squares down from line G and draw horizontal line H. This completes the basic grid you need to design "Bloomin' Grids" quilts.

Any horizontal line that ends to the right of line E and any vertical line that ends below line H is extraneous and may now be erased, or at least ignored for the rest of the design process. (See Diagram 6.)

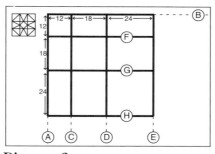

**Diagram 6**

Go over the basic grid lines (the heavy lines in Diagram 6) with a brightly colored pencil (like red or bright blue—some color that will contrast well with the pencil lines when seen through the tracing paper at a later stage of designing.) These colored lines will help you distinguish the basic blocks within the basic grid as you are drafting patterns into it. Now switch back to your regular lead pencil. The next step is to draft the traditional quilt block, in this case Doris's Delight,

into each of the 9 block units—squares and rectangles—within the basic grid. However, in order to see the curves come up across the entire grid, we are going to draft only a few lines at a time, working step-by-step across the entire grid, instead of drafting Doris's Delight completely, a block at a time. One of the keys to using "Bloomin' Grids" as a design tool is to *keep the total quilt surface in mind* at all times: (Sometimes we "can't see the forest for the trees" when we focus on individual blocks instead of the total quilt surface.)

First, indicate the major division lines: these are design lines that subdivide a patchwork block to create a 9-patch block, a 4-patch block, and so on. Since our example is a 9-patch pattern in which the major division lines are a part of the pattern itself, we need to divide the block into thirds. Lay your ruler on the paper to subdivide the first unit (in the upper left-hand corner of the basic grid) into thirds. Notice that you need to divide all the units below it into thirds as well. So draw your division lines from line B to line H, all the way down the basic grid. (See Diagram 7.)

Likewise, when you lay your ruler down to subdivide that corner unit horizontally into thirds, the same division applies to all the units

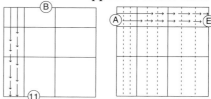

**Diagram 7**

to the right: Hence, draw your horizontal lines from line A to line E. Continue drawing in the major division lines throughout the basic grid in this manner.

The next step is to draft the rest

of the design lines from Doris's Delight into each block unit within the basic grid, again working step-by-step across the entire grid before completing the block within any single unit. First draw the diagonal lines only across the upper left and lower right patches throughout the grid. (See Diagram 8.)

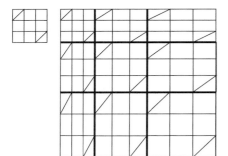

**Diagram 8**

Now go back and draft the other 2 corner patches. (See Diagram 9.) Now lift the paper and look at your design from different angles—top, bottom, from both sides, and especially from the corners (or on point), and you will see the curves and three-dimensional aspect of this design system come alive.

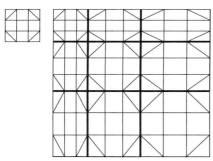

**Diagram 9**

Now draft the middle patches on the top and bottom of the block. When this process is complete, look at the paper from different angles again to see the designs that develop. (See Diagram 10.)

Next, draft the center patch in each unit. (See Diagram 11.) Notice the chain of patterns this creates across the pieced surface.

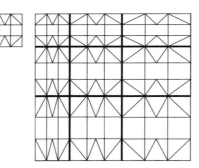

**Diagram 10**

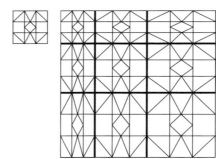

**Diagram 11**

Finally, draft the middle patches on the right and left sides of the block into each unit of the basic grid; the Doris's Delight pattern is now complete. (See Diagram 12.)

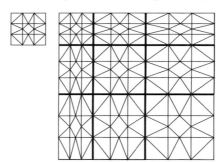

**Diagram 12**

*Note*: Although we drafted the entire block in this example, remember that one of your design options is to draft a traditional block only partially in the basic grid. Sometimes a more interesting overall design develops when you do not complete the block in each unit.

Take a second sheet of 11-inch by 17-inch graph paper from your pad. Choose another 9-patch pattern and draft it into the basic grid.

(Try your favorite 9-patch block, choose one from a sourcebook of patchwork patterns, or select one from the end of this chapter. Use the same divisions for the grid that we used for Doris's Delight. Those divisions were 12, 18, and 24 graph paper squares.)

Remember that the first step is to draft the pattern as a traditional square in the upper left-hand corner of your graph paper. If you choose a pattern that does not have the major division lines as part of the pattern (such as the blocks shown in Diagram 13), you will not automatically draw the division lines in as we did in drafting the pattern Doris's Delight.

**Diagram 13**

Instead, make "tick marks" on your colored lines to help you locate the major divisions of the block, but do not draw division lines across the entire grid. (See Diagram 14.)

*Note*: Another category of traditional patchwork patterns that produces delightful surprises with this "Bloomin' Grids" design technique is the 4-patch pattern. The procedure is the same as that which we used to draft Doris's Delight, but the measurements of the basic grid for 4-patch patterns are as follows: 16, 20, and 24 graph paper squares.

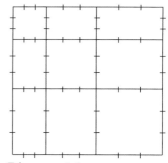

**Diagram 14**

## From Basic Grid to Total Design
### Surface: Rotations

Make "Bloomin' Grid" drawings based on as many 9-patch or 4-patch blocks as you like. Then choose your favorite and make 6 photocopies of your design. When you photocopy, you do not need to have the graph paper lines show, but be sure that your design lines are dark enough to photocopy well.

Trim away the margin from around 4 of your photocopies. Set the other 2 aside for now.

Letter the corners of each of the trimmed photocopies as in Diagram 15, with A in the corner with the smallest block unit, and then B, C, and D clockwise around the basic grid.

We are now going to look at a number of ways to combine these 4 photocopied elements into a total quilt design. For each rotation (the combination of 4 rotated elements), place your copies edge to edge on a cleared table, so it is easy to picture

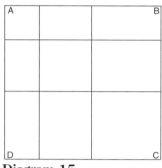

**Diagram 15**

the rotation as a total quilt design. Since you will want to view each rotation from the top, bottom, sides, and on point from different corners, choose a table space you can conveniently walk around. *Note*: Every rotation may not be a smashing design success, but going through many different rotations will give you an understanding of how the basic grid transforms the block, sparking ideas for other blocks you may want to try.

In the illustrations shown here, a small rotation schematic labeled with letters is shown below a larger grouping of 4 basic grids placed in that rotation. Lines on a second small schematic suggest the design movement generally achieved by that rotation. Though you will be using the same design for all of your rotations, designs based on 3 different blocks are used below to show you some of the striking effects that can be obtained using various blocks in the "Bloomin' Grids" basic grid.

For the first rotation, place 2 As and 2 Cs to the center, edge to edge, as shown in Diagram 16.

Notice that the A area is an intense design that seems to recede from the viewer, while the C area of the design is more open and appears to be closer to the viewer. Thus, this variation makes it look as if something is coming from 2 corners and "going over" the motif that has come from the opposite 2 corners.

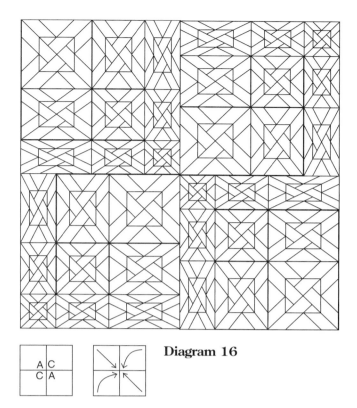

**Diagram 16**

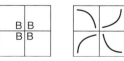

Next, place all Bs to the center. Notice that you are now placing 4 rectangles in the center, pinwheel style. (See Diagram 17.)

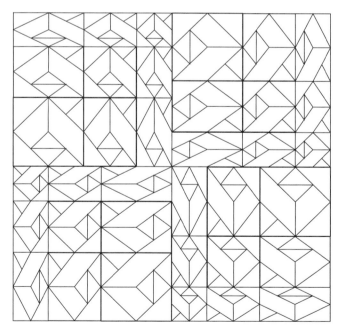

**Diagram 17**

Some sort of directional pinwheel or star usually emerges with this rotation. Notice also that not all major division lines—and thus key elements of the design—match up. Do not be afraid of this situation in "Bloomin' Grids" quilts—it can lead to some wonderful color strategies.

Next place Bs and Ds to the center. This rotation often yields an hourglass shape. (See Diagram 18.)

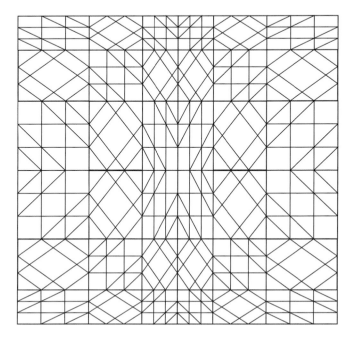

  **Diagram 19**

  **Diagram 18**

Now place all As to the center. (See Diagram 19.) This draws the most intense design to the center of the quilt and can cause a design dilemma if the lines that radiate from the center make the eye want to "zoom" off the edges of the piece. To control this distracting effect with color, make sure background values go from lighter in the center to dark at the edges to help determine the edge of the quilt.

Bring the most open design areas to the center by putting all the Cs to the center. This puts your most intense design around the outside edges, forming a sort of border with the design alone. This rotation, shown in Diagram 20, is the most three-dimensional of all those we have tried, and gives the illusion that there is a spherical shape under the center area of the pieced surface. This rotation gives the strongest illusion of curved lines over the pieced surface, even though there are no curved seams.

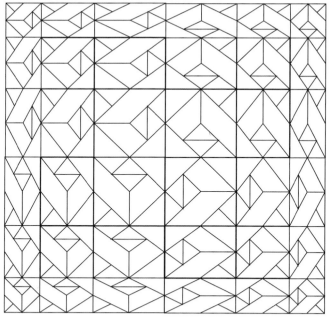

  **Diagram 20**

There are many other edge-to-edge rotations you might try, such as ones shown in Diagram 21. Experiment and discover the varying effects each offers.

 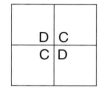 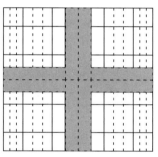

**Diagram 21**

In addition, try overlapping your 4 basic grids for even more design possibilities. Here is another example of the Cs-to-the-center rotation. Try overlapping the C units partially, along major division lines, or entirely, and watch the results. (See Diagram 22.)

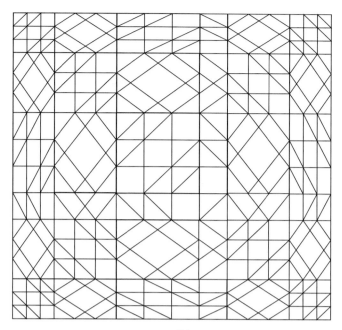

**Diagram 22b**
**Block units in C corner overlapping by ⅔ block (gray area).**

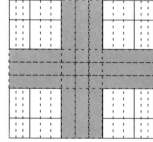

**Diagram 22c**
**Block units in C corner overlapping completely (gray area).**

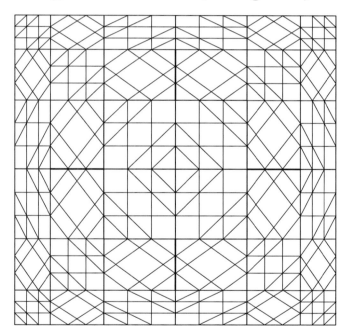

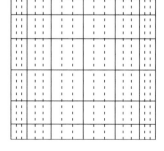

**Diagram 22a**
**Block units in C corner meeting edge to edge.**

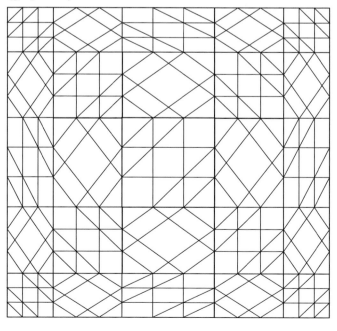

## Design Diversions

Many variations are possible in the "Bloomin' Grids" process. In my workshops, students often experiment by using more than 1 basic grid (from more than 1 traditional block) in rotations or by checkerboarding 2 different patchwork patterns in the same basic grid. (For more information on checkerboarding—especially on choosing patterns that "reach across" block borders to expand design possibilities—see my book *Blockbuster Quilts.*) You also can try leaving sections of the basic grid blank, to be filled by inventive piecing or appliqué. Asymmetrical blocks invite exploration, offering their own "special effects."

## Creating a Border

Once you have chosen a rotation of 4 basic grids, you have the option of adding another row or rows of units that are unrelated to the interior blocks, to act as a border. These units should be much narrower than the smallest block in the basic grid and, as such, are not broken up by as many lines as the interior units.

For the quilt *Sea Route,* for example, I drew a line 6 inches (6 squares on the graph paper) beyond the basic rotated units; then I extended major division lines from the basic grid and subdivided the new spaces to give the effect of a checkerboard border.

The diagonal lines crossing the checkerboard at a random angle were added in order to bring out the curves within the quilt, which had been camouflaged by the color strategy.

There are other ways of filling narrow border units. Draw a line beyond the rotated basic grid, extend the major division lines out to meet it, and fill in the resulting units with diagonals. (See Diagram 23.)

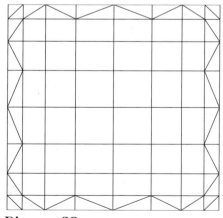

**Diagram 23**

In an extended example (see Diagram 24), 3 corner blocks from the basic grid were replaced by blocks

into which new design lines were drawn, extending the border design back into the body of the quilt. (See the gray areas in Diagram 24.)

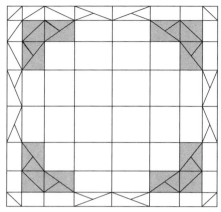

**Diagram 24**

## Blocks on Point

"Bloomin' Grids" sing yet another song when they are viewed not as a square quilt, but on point, as a diamond. To bring the basic grid on point out to a square shape, outline a square on graph paper that represents, to scale, the 4 basic grids in rotation. Then sketch in lines that represent the edge of the quilt. (See Diagram 25.)

Place tracing paper over this graph paper drawing and experiment with ways to fill in the blank corners. Diagram 26 shows 2 different corner-design possibilities. Note that my quilts *Bloomin' IV* and *Bloomin' V* (see pages 82 and 83) are basic grids turned on point.

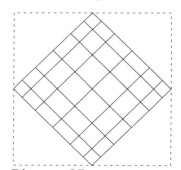

**Diagram 25**

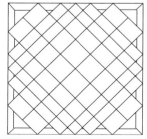

**Diagram 26**

*Sea Route*
59" x 59"
1986

In the quilt *Sea Route,* which appeared in *Blockbuster Quilts* (Bothell, WA: That Patchwork Place), the illusion of curves is not as marked, but it is accentuated by the lines superimposed on the checkerboard border, which create unexpected angles.

## Now to the Fabric: Making the Puzzle Board

Now it is time to bring your fabric samples into the design process. Choose your favorite rotation design and, using rubber cement, stick the 4 basic grids flush with one another in that design on your posterboard, about 1 inch from one corner. (Rubber cement is used because it does not distort the paper.) These 4 basic grids now form a single pieced surface, a "puzzle board," on which you are going to cut and glue fabric pieces to fill in the pieces of the puzzle.

Trim around the puzzle board, leaving at least a 1-inch margin. On the remaining posterboard, rubber-cement one of the 2 remaining photocopies of your "Bloomin' Grid" to cut into templates. The sixth photocopy will serve as your reference guide.

### Marking the Reference Guide

On this reference guide, label each of the 9 units as in Diagram 27. (*Note*: Use capital "H" and lower case "i" to avoid confusion later when templates are cut apart. When I is turned on its side, it resembles H.)

|   |   |   |
|---|---|---|
| A | B | C |
| D | E | F |
| G | H | i |

**Diagram 27**

Label the pieces within each unit. Corresponding pieces will have the same number in each unit, but different letters, denoting their units. (See Diagram 28.)

### Marking the Templates

Next, letter and number the template sheet just like the reference guide sheet. *Do not cut out templates yet!*

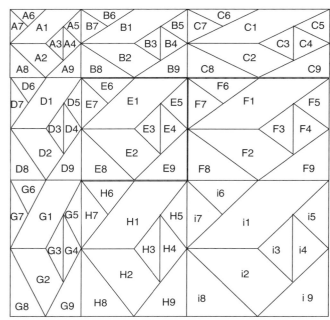

**Diagram 28**

### Color Strategies

There are many different color strategies that can be applied to the "Bloomin' Grids" quilts, and each strategy will make the pieced surface look different. It might even disguise the fact that the quilts are all from the same templates! Successful color strategies are more easily attainable if—first, you always keep the *total pieced surface* in mind, and second, you think about *sprinkling light* across that surface, rather than agonizing about which color goes here or there.

To work with color strategies, it is important to think of your fabrics as values (light, light-medium, medium, dark-medium, and dark) rather than as *colors* (red, blue, green). *Hint*: This takes years of practice. The more you work at it, the better you will become.

In the following strategies, remember that if the diagram says "light" in a certain area, that doesn't mean that there are *no* mediums or even darks in that area. Sometimes you need a little of a darker value to offset the lightness of another and vice-versa. Also, just because you start out attempting one color strategy, don't be afraid to abandon it if some other wonderful play of color begins to emerge in your quilt. These color strategies are merely jumping-off places, strategies to help you cut and put up that first piece of fabric—and then the second, then the third.

With each color strategy presented below, there is a fabric mockup to suggest how that strategy might be implemented.

## Lights at the Top

For your first strategy, pretend that there is a fluorescent tube across the top of your quilt and that its light fades as the eye reaches the bottom of the quilt. Therefore, you should keep most of your light values at the top of the piece, gradually adding medium values and finally using your darkest values at the bottom edge of the quilt. (*Note:* Whenever you are trying to move from lights in one area to darks in another, cut out a few light pieces and glue them in place; then cut a few very dark ones and glue them on the puzzle board. It will then be easier to find the values that belong in between.)

## Spine of Light

In this strategy, pretend that there is a shaft of light that falls vertically down the center of your quilt and that the light weakens as you move out to each edge of the quilt.

## Central Focus of Light

Pretend that there is a spotlight hitting the center of your quilt. Now your lightest values will be concentrated in the center of the quilt. Values will gradually darken evenly as you approach the edges of your quilt. This would be an especially effective strategy for the Cs-in-the-center rotation described above. (See page 88.)

To vary this theme, pretend that the spotlight is striking your quilt off-center. Now the light fabrics will still be concentrated in a certain area, but that area will not be in the center as it was in the previous strategy.

## Light to Dark Along the Diagonal

For this strategy, visualize a flood lamp just off one corner of the quilt. Choose very light values for that corner and very dark ones for the opposite corner. The remaining corners should be medium to dark-medium in value.

Or, make your light values form a spine of light that extends from corner to corner; then gradually add the light-mediums, mediums, dark-mediums, and finally darks as you work out to the opposite corners.

## Applying Color Strategies

Before beginning to cut fabric pieces, take a moment to study your puzzle board. Motifs may begin to jump out at you—such as circles, diamonds, cloverleaf designs, crosses, or Maltese crosses, to name only a few. These may appear as centralized motifs or may repeat across the design surface.

To be able to pick out motifs more easily, tape your puzzle board to the wall. Lightly tape a piece of tracing paper over your puzzle board and, with a colored pencil, see how many different motifs—either centralized or repeated—you can find. Use several pieces of tracing paper, because the longer you work with the puzzle board, the more motifs you generally find.

The key to maximizing the design value of your "Bloomin' Grids" puzzle board is to look for motifs that cross block lines: That is, look for motifs that camouflage where one block stops and the next one begins and emphasize that situation with color. (See Diagrams 29 and 30.)

If you have a motif that repeats from the center to the edge of the puzzle board, for instance, you might use your lightest values only in the smallest version of that motif; in the next largest motif, use somewhat darker values, and so on until you are using your darkest values at the edge of the quilt.

Or you might use very light values in the smallest version of the motif, very dark values in the next larger version, and then alternate very light and very dark values until you get to the edge of the quilt.

Another graphic mechanism is a motif that scatters across the surface. Try applying one color strategy to the motifs (for example, light in the middle to dark at the outer edge of the quilt) and the opposite strategy to the background behind those motifs (dark in the middle to light at the outside edge).

Since you can take almost any color strategy, apply it to the puzzle board you have designed, and create a successful quilt, don't worry too much about the "best" strategy at this point. Choose one and start cutting the pieces!

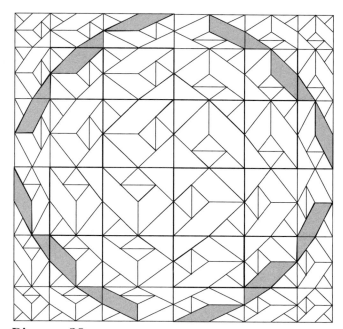

**Diagram 29**

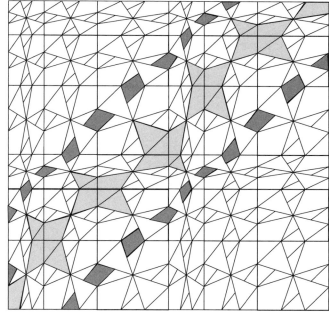

**Diagram 30**

## Beginning the Actual Mockup

To bring your puzzle board to life, you will need fabric scissors and rotary cutting equipment, your template sheet (backed with posterboard), and your reference guide. Arrange your fabrics (backed with index cards) in front of you in a long overlapping line of cards that move from lightest values to darkest.

Before cutting any templates apart, it is important to prepare a table space for them. In the process of cutting fabric pieces for the mockup, you must keep the templates organized and easy to retrieve. Therefore, label 9 pieces of typing paper A-i and place them on your work table as trays for the templates for each grid unit.

Next, cut the template sheet apart *into block units only* (A-i)—do not cut out any individual templates until you actually need them. Place the block units on their appropriate paper trays on your work table.

Now you are ready to cut out the first fabric puzzle piece for your puzzle board. Don't panic! If the job seems overwhelming, you may need to choose only one shape (perhaps a triangle, as in the illustration at right) and complete your color strategy (light to dark) in that shape only; then go back and choose a couple of other shapes to use in the same way.

To cut out a particular puzzle piece, determine which template you need by using your reference guide, which can be rotated to match your puzzle board. Cut that template out of its respective block unit with the rotary cutter and the Plexiglas straightedge.

Hold the template right side up on the fabric and trim around the template with your paper scissors.

(Accuracy is important only because you don't want to leave spaces between the pieces on the puzzle board. And since you are holding the template and trimming around it, you are cutting the puzzle piece large enough to insure that the background will be covered.) *Be sure to return the template to its proper place on the table as soon as you are through cutting it out.*

Then put a small amount of glue from a glue stick onto the index card backing of the shape you have cut out and glue it in place on the puzzle board. (Use only a small amount of glue so that you can easily move a piece if you change your mind about color placement.)

*The key to color placement is: Don't be paralyzed by indecision— jump in and try it!* You can *think* about your color strategy and *wonder* whether a given fabric is going to work in a given area all day long. But until you cut it out and put it in place to see what happens, you won't know for sure.

As you are working, step back from your work often to look at it from a distance—this will help you evaluate the overall movement of values. In addition, look at your work through a reducing glass, through the wrong end of binoculars, or through a security peephole (such as hardware stores sell), to distance yourself even further from your work. If you have none of the above tools, at least step back as far as you can and squint at your puzzle board. This will enable you to see more value and less color in the overall design.

Continue cutting, placing, and gluing fabric shapes until your entire puzzle board is covered and your mockup is complete.

## From Mockup to Full-Size Quilt

One of the advantages of using 8 squares-to-the-inch graph paper is that designs easily translate to a full-size quilt. Let 1 small square on the graph paper equal 1 square inch full-size. In this way, a quilt mockup that measures 96 graph paper squares can be translated into an 96-inch by 96-inch quilt. If this is too large, determine how large a half-scale (1 square = ½ inch) quilt would be by dividing the total measurement in half, or, in this case, 48 inches—small wall hanging size.

If 48 inches is too small, one option is to add a row of blocks, perhaps 6 inches beyond the 48-inch perimeter, to make a 60-inch quilt. Before committing to this plan, draft your most complex block full-size as a 6-inch square, to see first if it is feasible to piece, and second, if it adds to the design of the total quilt. My quilt *Beyond the Bandbox* has an additional row of blocks around the outside edge; the corner blocks are 6 inches square.

If adding another row of blocks is not appropriate, try using a more simplified version of the block (leaving some design lines out), substituting another block, or filling in the units with a checkerboard or other simple division of the space.

If you do not want a square quilt, you have a couple of options. Add one or more rows of units to make a rectangular quilt with the desired measurements; or begin with the measurements of the quilt you want and create the unit blocks within it. Obviously the rotations would not be performed in the same manner, but having already played with rotations, you will be able to plug in design units from the rotations to achieve the desired design effects.

To make the quilt, you will need

*Beyond the Bandbox*
59" x 59"
1986

This quilt was made from the same templates as those used for *Sea Route* (see page 91), but here the checkerboard border has been replaced by an additional row of blocks.

to letter and number the templates involved just as we did in the mockup example above. But this time you will have 2 guide sheets: one in a square format to indicate the basic units and another in the rectangular format to indicate location of those basic units throughout the whole surface.

## Making Full-Size Templates

Once you have arrived at a layout, whether it is the full-size translation of the drawing (96 inches square, in our example above), a half-size translation, or a rectangular quilt, you can make the full-size templates. Remember that you need full-size templates for only the basic grid. Those same block units

repeat over the entire surface.

Determine the full-size of the basic grid required by your quilt plan and the full-size required of each unit within the grid. Draft each unit full-size and spray-adhesive or rubber-cement each to a piece of posterboard. *Letter and number all templates* as on the template guide sheet.

Follow the same procedure for keeping templates in order as was explained in the mockup section: Keep all A templates in one pile, B templates in another, etc.

## Cutting Out Fabric

To make a full-size quilt, it is very helpful to place the cut fabric pieces on a vertical design surface. You may want to attach markers made of ribbons or pearl cotton threads on the design surface first to indicate rough divisions of the quilt, especially if you are going to start by plugging in 1 shape across the entire surface. (See Diagram 31.)

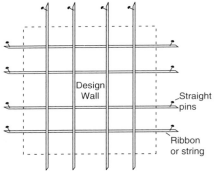

**Diagram 31**

"Bloomin' Grid" designs may require that you modify your usual method of marking and cutting fabric shapes. When you begin to change the angles in a quilt, you may find yourself using very elongated shapes or uniquely shaped triangles. These shapes may not lend themselves well to being cut out with the seam allowance already added to them and then being sewn together using the presser foot of your sewing machine as a seam guide.

The piecing process is made simpler and it requires less time for ripping out if you proceed as though you were hand piecing. When you select a template, cut it out of its block unit with a rotary cutter, turn it over, and trace around it on the *wrong side* of the fabric, with a pencil. Since the line you traced is your *sewing line,* when you cut out the shape, you must add a seam allowance beyond this traced line. (See Diagram 32.)

An important detail, which will make piecing of odd shapes easier, is being aware of grain line when you cut. In any given shape in your quilt, only one edge can be on grain, or parallel to the threads of the fabric. This edge will have the least amount of stretching and distortion during the piecing process. When cutting a new shape, note whether a given edge will be sewn to a straight grain or an off-grain edge. Always try to sew a straight grain to an off-grain edge, for ease of piecing and for the most stability of the finished pieced surface.

Do not sew any pieces together until all pieces are cut out, since you may change your mind about colors chosen as the quilt design work progresses on the wall.

When you are ready to sew 1 shape to another, you have 2 sewing lines to pin together and can sew accurately by machine. Place pins *along the sewing line*, not perpendicular to it. Place the first pin at the *exact* beginning of one sewing line, another pin from the other side at the exact end of the sewing line; add pins in between as needed.

When sewing an area in which many points come together, do not sew from raw edge to raw edge of the fabrics, but rather from seam line beginning to seam line ending. This will leave seam allowances free to be fanned clockwise or counterclockwise on the back of the pieced surface for the best distribution of bulk.

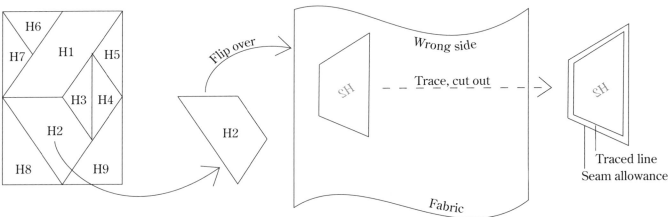

**Diagram 32**

### Richness of Surface

Many of the block units (and thus individual shapes within them) are quite large. This is a good opportunity to enrich the pieced surface by using more than 1 fabric within any given shape (triangle, etc.).

Even if the shapes in your quilt are not oversized, a good motto is *"Never use 2 fabrics when you can use 20!"* If there are only 2 or 3 fabrics in a given quilt, it is obvious when 1 fabric really doesn't go well with 1 of the other 2. If there are 20 different fabrics in the same quilt, the eye blends the colors together in the overall surface, and no 1 fabric stands out as a misfit.

Moreover, you can use very simple shapes in "Bloomin' Grids" and other quilts, and still achieve great visual complexity by strip-piecing or checkerboarding fabric and cutting templates out of that pieced fabric.

For example, in *Bloomin' VI* there are only 2 pieced blocks used to create the design: 1 block in the center and another block in the rest of the block units of the basic grid. This latter block is very simple, being composed of only 6 triangles. To create the fabrics in the blocks, strips of 2 or 3 fabrics were sewn together, and then the triangle templates were cut from the assembled fabrics.

*Bloomin' VI*
70" x 70"
1991

This quilt has two different patchwork patterns, one in the center block units, another in all other block units. The visual complexity in this quilt comes from strip piecing: cutting any given template out of several fabrics that have been previously sewn together, rather than out of a single fabric.

In the quilt *Visions,* the central square (or rectangle) of each block was cut from a checkerboard in which color placement was random. The checkerboard, formed with strip-piecing techniques, was altered slightly in the rectangular shapes so that there could be a 4-unit by 4-unit checkerboard in each block.

Do not be afraid of large-size blocks. The center block of *Visions* measures 24 inches square; but, as you see, strip-piecing techniques add visual complexity to a surface, allowing you to use very large (and easily pieced) templates to create your "Bloomin' Grids" quilt.

## Quilting Designs

Remembering that the focus for "Bloomin' Grids" quilts is to reach for the unexpected, you should plan quilting designs that flow over the total surface. These will be more effective than quilting designs that merely follow seam lines. In devising the quilting pattern, there are many ways to take advantage of the complex graphic surfaces that are presented by these quilts. For example, look for areas where the new angles seem to suggest curves or circles and then quilt actual curves and circles in that area. Also find areas where motifs cross 2 or more blocks; highlight those motifs with the quilting lines.

To experiment with quilting-line designs, place successive pieces of tracing paper over either the mockup or the puzzle board and challenge yourself to draw very different kinds of quilting lines onto the tracing papers.

*Visions*
84" x 84"
1987

This quilt could be perceived as an aerial view of little stools with checkerboard seats, covering a globe. Note the placement of lights and darks in the "legs" of the stools, and the subtle changing of the shape of the checkerboards.

## Blocks to Try

Here are a few 4-patch and 9-patch blocks that you may want to try singly or in combination in "Bloomin' Quilt Grids" designs. Many more choices are shown in quilt reference books, some of which are listed below.

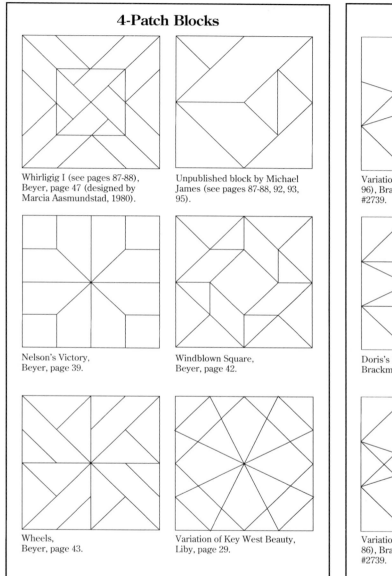

### 4-Patch Blocks

Whirligig I (see pages 87-88), Beyer, page 47 (designed by Marcia Aasmundstad, 1980).

Unpublished block by Michael James (see pages 87-88, 92, 93, 95).

Nelson's Victory, Beyer, page 39.

Windblown Square, Beyer, page 42.

Wheels, Beyer, page 43.

Variation of Key West Beauty, Liby, page 29.

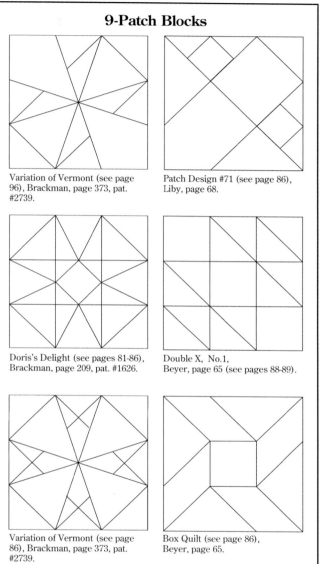

### 9-Patch Blocks

Variation of Vermont (see page 96), Brackman, page 373, pat. #2739.

Patch Design #71 (see page 86), Liby, page 68.

Doris's Delight (see pages 81-86), Brackman, page 209, pat. #1626.

Double X, No.1, Beyer, page 65 (see pages 88-89).

Variation of Vermont (see page 86), Brackman, page 373, pat. #2739.

Box Quilt (see page 86), Beyer, page 65.

## Bibliography

Beyer, Jinny. *The Quilter's Album of Blocks and Borders.* McLean, VA: EPM Publications, 1980.

Brackman, Barbara. *An Encyclopedia of Pieced Quilt Patterns.* Lawrence, KS: Prairie Flower Publishing, 1984.

Liby, Shirley. *Exploring Four Patch.* Self-published, 812 W. Cromer, Muncie, IN 47303, 1987.

Miller, Margaret J. *Blockbuster Quilts.* Bothell, WA: That Patchwork Place, 1991.

# Quilts That Speak Aloud

Some quilts have rich stories to tell. Others offer only whispered clues about the time, the place, and the quilter from whom they came. Marta Amundson's quilts, however, speak out in clear, vibrant tones, expressing their maker's concerns about our earth and how we live on it.

*Quilt with the Best* visited Marta in spring 1991, at her farm near the Wind River Mountains, in a valley under the wide Wyoming sky. From their remodeled farmhouse, filled with art and antiques and framed by lilac and sagebrush, Marta and her husband, Larry, look out over Ocean Lake and its pelicans, great blue herons, and Arctic terns. The perimeter of the lake is an important habitat for many kinds of water birds, as well as raptors such as eagles, hawks, and owls. "Sometimes we see egrets and ibis in our yard," Marta says. " We also have western grebes and American avocets—a not-so-common shore bird with a salmon-colored head, black-and-white wings, and a long, upturned bill."

"Living in a place like this," Marta continues, "I have a lot of time to read and think about what's going on in the world." Environmental issues are never far from her thoughts. "I don't think you can live in Wyoming and not have strong feelings and concerns about the environment."

Educated in Sweden at the University of Stockholm and at Albion College in Michigan, Marta graduated magna cum laude with a B.A. in visual art and art history. She moved to Wyoming in 1976. "I've lived in the West a good long while, and I've always believed that nature is important and deserves safeguarding. Some people say, 'What does it matter if one kind of fish is gone?' It matters a lot to me."

*I want a voice in the world, and my quilts give me that voice.*

Marta's concerns, and the images that express them, are played out in a variety of crafts, including quilting, stained glass, and pottery. "For the past ten years," she tells us, "I have created stained glass windows for public and private buildings. In that time, I've been fortunate to have some fine teachers who gave me a sense of color and design that can be carried from one medium to another." Marta's quilts relate very closely to her windows; both windows and quilts depend on the interplay of organic and geometric shapes, and she likes to use solid, brilliant colors in her quilts that make them seem glass-like.

"Sometimes, in making my quilts, I feel as though I'm working in glass without the glass. Both crafts require precision and exactness; both reward the tedious work involved with the pleasure of seeing the concept realized. However, because the materials of quiltmaking are much less expensive than glass, there's a greater freedom to experiment." Also, there is less of the pressure of permanence. "When I make a quilt, I am making an item that will last a long time, but probably not as long as the windows of a church or public building. I feel more free, too, because I need not be concerned with integrating the piece into a given architecture."

Although Marta has made quilts for beds and babies since 1978, she never thought of her own quilting as art until she began her Menagerie series in 1989. Menagerie, a series of quilts combining traditional patchwork with Marta's original animal designs, was created to increase public awareness of environmental and cultural issues.

"My quilts have a mixture of themes," she says.

"Some of them point out serious issues, like the dangers to sea turtles, blue whales, and many other species posed by predation or loss of habitat. Other quilts offer humorous views of common human predicaments: You may see your own experience in some of the pieces." In *Search for the Cat's Meow,* for example, Marta explores "the way we all try to some extent to please our peers with the clothes we wear and the way we act. The piece is dedicated to my girls, Julie and Torrey, who have raised grooming rituals to an art form."

Marta's husky, Natasha, sits among a pile of quilts. The two quilts hung on the fence are *If Wishes Were Horses* (at left) and *Just Call Me Fredrick* (at right).

Having a sense of humor, Marta says, "helps me cope with that part of life that is unfair, ridiculous, or hard to rationalize. However, there's an irony in my work that is very pointed and serious."

In each quilt, Marta likes to combine traditional patterns with a unique color harmony. The animals quilted in the wide, plain border relate to the quilt's theme. Marta takes advantage of quick-piecing and rotary cutting techniques to make the geometric center section. To evenly space her animal designs on the borders, she cuts multiple images from freezer paper and irons them in place. Marta quilts four to six hours each day and has completed 22 quilts in the last year and a half.

After basting and marking a quilt, Marta likes to sit in an old mission-style rocker with strong, wide arms. "With jazz on the stereo, my needle glides across the chalk lines. Quilting gives me time to sort out my own ideas about my work, my family, and my life."

Of her work, Marta says, "I want a voice in the world, and my quilts give me that voice. I think that in a lot of ways women feel a sense of powerlessness. Making quilts with political, environmental, or cultural statements gives me that power back. When my quilts are exhibited, both men and women show a great deal of interest. My quilts encourage people to slow down and to think about our daily lives—what we're doing to ourselves and to our environment."

To focus attention on the issues, Marta keeps the design of each quilt simple. "I have a wild imagination, and I could make phantasmagoric quilt surfaces, but I don't choose to do that. I want people to feel comfortable with the designs and be drawn to the colors and the traditional associations. Then I hope they will think about the issues related to each quilt."

The floor-to-ceiling windows in the dining room of Marta's home include one of her stained glass panels, depicting a great blue heron. Clear glass windows look out on Ocean Lake, home to many birds, including herons, Canada geese, and cranes.

To emphasize her ideas, Marta displays her quilts with artist's statements beside each one. (Some of these statements accompany pictures of the quilts in the following pages.) The statements are printed in large type on letter-sized paper. Quilt viewers can read the titles from 15 feet away. Marta's sister, Angela Kantola, helps develop the statements, and her step-mother, Char Griner, prints them on her computer in large type for Marta's shows.

"I'm not trying to be controversial. My goal is not necessarily to change anyone's mind, but to point out issues that deserve thought and action. If my quilts bring these issues to people's attention and they spend a little time thinking about them, I feel successful," Marta says.

Animal images and environmental themes also appear in Marta's ceramics. Once a year, she takes a holiday from stained glass and quilting and travels to Richard Leach's studio in Michigan, where she spends a few busy weeks making pottery. "Clay—now there's a material that you can really put your hands in," she says. "Throwing pieces, feeling the clay move through my hands—that's my recreation, my once-a-year vacation from being technical and precise. It's a time to cleanse myself by working really hard and fast." It's an intense form of play, Marta admits. "It's like mountaineering. You feel best afterwards, in the shower!"

Still another creative venture is her Art to Wear series of quilted garments, including vests made on a shape by Yvonne Porcella and Seminole jackets. (See page 102.) Her newest wearables are reversible jackets structured like the *hippari* worn by Japanese field workers. In addition to teaching quilt workshops that focus on color theory and rapid construction methods, Marta offers pieced-garment workshops that give more immediate satisfaction to students but still expose them to color theory. "It's important to understand how colors act on each other and how they can be used to create space and definition. For the novice quiltmaker, color selection seems to be the greatest mystery. I like to give my students the confidence to make good choices for their own work."

> *I'm not trying to be controversial. My goal is not necessarily to change anyone's mind, but to point out issues that deserve thought and action. If my quilts bring these issues to people's attention and they spend a little time thinking about them, I feel successful.*

## WOLVES AT THE DOOR

Ranchers nearly eliminated predators from all or parts of their natural range in Wyoming. Only after these animals had almost disappeared did we begin to understand the consequences of our actions and the need to restore them to their natural habitats. Now, after many years of opposition, public sentiment generally supports reintroducing the gray wolf to Yellowstone. The controversy now centers on how the wolves will be managed once they are brought back. Although it will be a tough political battle, it's only a matter of time until the controversy will be resolved and wolves will return to the Yellowstone ecosystem.

*Wolves at the Door*
40" x 49"
1990

I don't think you can live in Wyoming and not have concerns about the environment.

## OUTNUMBERED BY LITTLE FOXES

Sometimes the little problems in my life become so numerous that I become engulfed by them all. Alone, they might seem trivial, but as these little problems multiply, they wash over me like a wave, until I can no longer swim, but only cough and sputter. Thus, I stand as a rabbit surrounded by famished foxes.

*Outnumbered by Little Foxes,* 44" x 51", 1989

*Mountain Mirage,* Wyoming School for the Deaf, 111" x 55", 1985

Platter:
*The Homecoming*
14"
1990

> *Some people say,*
> *"What does it matter if one*
> *kind of fish is gone?"*
> *It matters a lot to me.*

## TURTLE SOUP

Sea turtle numbers have been decimated worldwide in the last few centuries by overhunting for meat, eggs, oil, and decorative objects. In the United States, sea turtles are protected from hunting, but still are threatened by drowning in shrimp trawls, alteration of nesting beaches, and predation. Recent laws mandating the use of turtle excluder devices (commonly called TEDs) should reduce drownings in shrimp trawls off the U.S. coast; however, enforcing their use is difficult. Hunting of turtles and their eggs continues in some countries, and, if left unchecked, will cause further decline of sea turtles and, ultimately, the disappearance of these unique species. Aware consumers can act to reduce the demand for sea turtle products by not purchasing them while traveling in the Caribbean and abroad.

*Turtle Soup*
42" x 49", 1990

*Turtle Soup,* detail

## AND THEN THERE WERE NONE

I'll never forget the excitement at our farm on Ocean Lake when we spotted a whooping crane for the first time. Larry first saw her in September of 1984. She flew over with a group of sandhill cranes so close that he could almost touch her. Each day for three weeks we put aside our tasks for the day until we could see her in the field glasses. The coffeepot worked overtime for the many biologists who waited with anticipation for the once-in-a-lifetime experience of getting a look. When a large group of sandhill cranes left to fly south in mid-October, they took our "Ms. Whooper" with them. She returned in April of 1985 and spent the spring and summer with us. When the cold came in October, she was gone and has not returned.

The whooping crane has been on the endangered species list since 1967. Although only 23 remained in 1941, co-operative recovery efforts by the United States and Canada have resulted in a total population that now exceeds 230 birds.

*And Then There Were None*
43" x 50", 1990

The flying crane used in the quilting of this piece was designed by Sylvia Long of Scottsdale, Arizona.

*And Then There Were None,* detail

## DON'T WAIT FOR PINKERTON

In 1989, my husband and I saw the opera *Madame Butterfly* with our 19-year-old daughter, Torrey. While I accepted the story as a classic tragedy, Torrey was perplexed. After the opera, she asked me, "Why did Madame Butterfly wait for Pinkerton all of those years? Why didn't she just get on with her life?" It seems sometimes we waste our lives waiting for men in one way or another. This quilt symbolizes good advice for women of all generations. Our lives are precious and finite. We must grasp every opportunity, not allow men to limit them!

*Don't Wait for Pinkerton,* 41" x 56", 1989

*Sometimes, in making my quilts, I feel as though I'm working in glass without the glass. Both crafts require precision and exactness; both reward the tedious work involved with the pleasure of seeing the concept realized. But because the materials are much less expensive in quiltmaking, there's a greater sense of freedom to experiment.*

*Hoppin' Good Time*
46" x 46", 1989

## HOPPIN' GOOD TIME

Linus Van Pelt once said that there is no problem too big or too complicated that it can't be run away from. Surely he must be right! Australia is the place in my mind where I go to daydream and escape the stress of day-to-day life.

*Silk Purse from a Sow's Ear*
42" x 45", 1990

## SILK PURSE FROM A SOW'S EAR

I made this quilt from fabric pieces carefully saved from years of sewing. Living in this area of sparse goods and population, I've learned by necessity to use every scrap of material. In Wyoming, the customs of the American throwaway society are not practical. Shopping for even slightly unusual items must be done by mail order or during the rare pilgrimage to the big city. Wyoming merchants feel that if you can't find what you want in their store, you can probably do without it.

Chapel window, Wyoming Sanitarium, 56" x 100", 1984

*My quilts have a mixture of themes. Some point out serious issues. Some are humorous views of common human predicaments: You may see your own experience in some of the pieces.*
*All my quilts encourage people to slow down and to think about our daily lives— what we're doing to ourselves and to our environment.*

Platter: *Return to the Thames*
13"
1990

## WHEN PIGS HAVE WINGS

This quilt is about those times when I just can't compromise anymore—when people have pushed me to my limit and I make the decision to stand my ground until *pigs have wings!*

Instructions and patterns for making this piece appear in *Great American Quilts 1992* (Oxmoor House, 1991).

*When Pigs Have Wings*
43" x 47"
1990

# Marta Amundson's Strip-Pieced Collar with Seminole Ribbons

This strip-pieced collar is among Marta Amundson's favorite simple teaching projects. It is accented by one of her original quilting designs, an osprey in flight. The project requires only a small investment of time and materials but produces a piece that quilters can wear with pride.

In stitching this piece, students can practice several techniques, including strip piecing, hand quilting, and a form of Seminole patchwork made with ribbons. (See the ribbon-trimmed patchwork accent across the back of the piece—opposite page.) "I like working with the Seminole patchwork technique," Marta says, "but I've found that an easier way to create patterns is to make a 'striped' fabric by gluing lengths of ribbon across a piece of fabric, cutting the fabric into pieces, and resewing." The ribbons also add a textural effect and a shimmer of satin to the finished patchwork strip.

In the summer of 1991, Marta and two assistants taught this collar at Camp Pinecliffe in Harrison, Maine. It was part of an arts-and-crafts program that included quilting, basketmaking, weaving, origami, bead necklaces, crayon batik, and photography. During the program, 28 girls made quilt block pillows. The seven campers pictured here went on to make strip-pieced collars. "With 156 children in and out of the arts-and-crafts room," Marta notes, "I didn't allow the campers to use the rotary cutter. For safety reasons, I cut their strips for them. We had four ancient sewing machines to work with, and the kids really gave them a workout!"

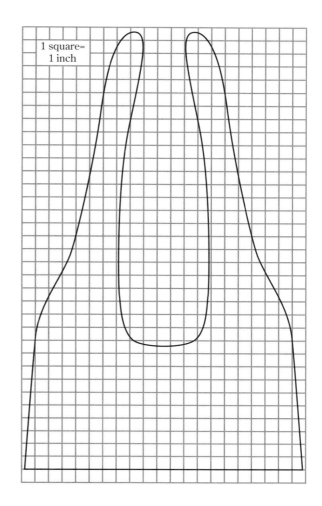

1 square=
1 inch

## Tools and Materials

Gather the following tools and supplies:

Sewing machine, iron

Rotary cutter, mat, and acrylic quilters' ruler, marked with 45-degree angle

Pinking shears, pins, and needles

Prewashed fabrics, including:

⅝ yard of white diaper flannel (heavier than regular flannel) for foundation fabric for collar

A variety (up to 10) of ¼-yard cuts of 100-percent cotton solids in harmonizing colors. (In choosing colors, think in terms of value. Pick 1 light value and 1 dark and pull other fabrics from the medium range. Include 1 bright color for sparkle and don't rule out dull colors—they may provide the foil that makes the combination of colors work. In our collar, for example, the dull green provides the direct complement to the vivid pink because they are opposite on the color wheel.)

⅝ yard of cotton chamois cloth for collar backing

Sewing thread to match chamois backing

"Invisible" nylon monofilament sewing thread

Quilting thread

¼-inch-wide satin ribbon: 1⅓ yards each of 2 harmonizing colors

Freezer paper, chalk pencil

## Make Foundation and Strip-Piece Fabric

Enlarge the collar pattern and use it to cut a foundation collar from the white diaper flannel.

Make a band of striped fabric to use in covering a portion of the foundation collar as follows: Using the rotary cutter, acrylic ruler, and mat, cut strips of fabric of varying widths from your cotton solids, cutting each piece across the width of the fabric.

Join the strips with ¼-inch seams, until you have a striped fabric that is 45 inches long and at least 12 inches wide. Press from the wrong side, pressing all seam allowances in the same direction, with this exception: Press seam allowances away from lighter fabrics, so that they will not show through on the right side of the collar. Set the band of striped fabric aside.

### Make Seminole Strip

Now choose a fabric in a color that works well with the ribbon colors and cut a strip 3½ inches wide across the width of that fabric. Place the ribbons ¼ inch apart, centered and parallel, on the fabric strip and mark the positions of the ribbons with pins at each end of the fabric strip. Coat the back of each ribbon with a washout glue stick.

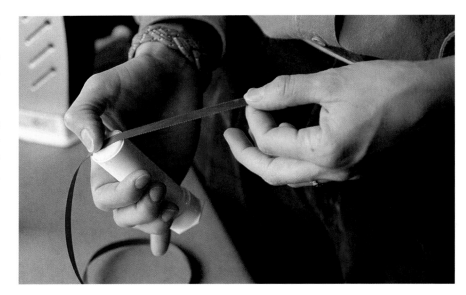

Glue the ribbons in place. Press the strip.

Fold the ribbon strip in half *widthwise,* with wrong sides facing. Make sure that the ribbons on each half of the strip are perfectly aligned with each other. Using the 45-degree marker on the acrylic ruler for positioning, make diagonal cuts across both layers of the folded strip, every 1½ inches. Cutting the folded strip will yield mirror-image pairs of 1½-inch-wide pieces.

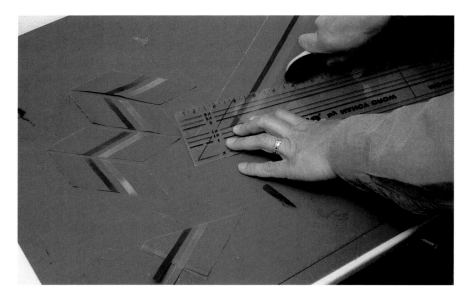

Join the fabric pairs with ¼-inch seams into a long patchwork strip, in which the ribbons connect in a zigzag pattern.

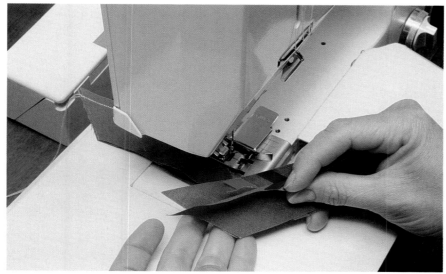

As you sew each pair of pieces together, check to see that the ribbons meet at the seam line.

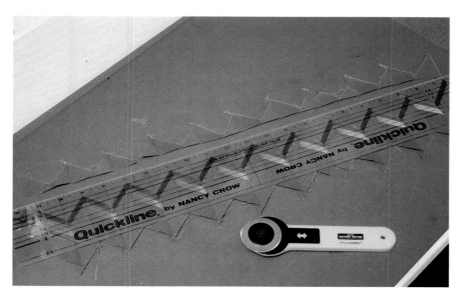

Trim the long, jagged edges away from each side of the patchwork strip.

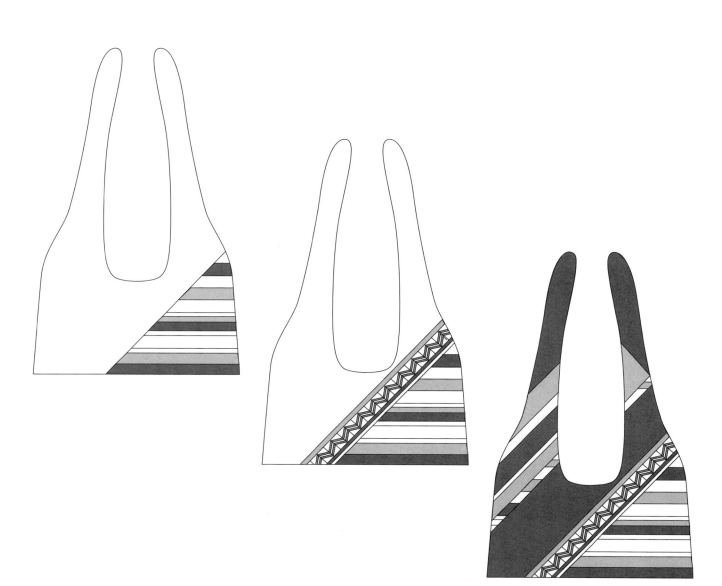

## Strip-Piece Collar

Using the 45-degree angle to position the ruler, cut a section from the striped fabric band you created earlier.

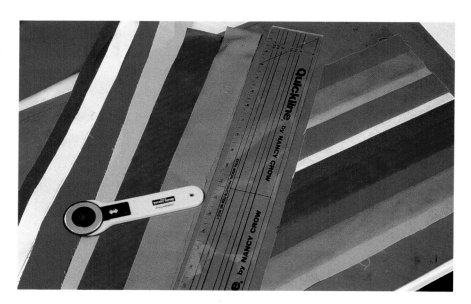

Place the striped fabric section over the lower right corner of your foundation collar. Place a narrow strip of fabric (fuchsia in photo) on the newly cut edge of the striped band, with right sides facing and raw edges aligned. For an extra dimensional effect, fold and press in half a second narrow strip of fabric (light pink). Insert it, aligning raw edges, between the striped band and the fuchsia fabric strip. Join, stitching through all layers, including foundation fabric. Flip the fuchsia strip over to the right side and press it in place.

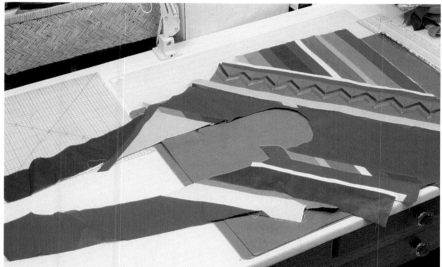

With right sides facing and raw edges aligned, place the Seminole strip along the fuchsia strip. Join with ¼-inch seam. Flip the Seminole strip over and press it in place. Continue strip-piecing on the foundation collar, using fabric strips (including a piece large enough to accommodate the quilted osprey design) and pieces of the striped fabric, until the foundation collar is completely covered. (*Note:* Before joining any new strip, flip it over to make sure it will be long enough to cover the foundation collar once it is sewn and turned.)

Place the chamois fabric right side up on the cutting mat. Cover the chamois with the pieced collar, turned right side down. Following the outline of the foundation collar, with the rotary cutter, trim away the excess strip piecing and cut out the chamois backing for the collar in one operation.

**Finish Collar**

With the chamois backing and strip-pieced collar right sides facing, stitch around the outer edges with a ¼-inch seam, leaving a 3-inch opening for turning at the base of the collar.

Pink the seam allowances and turn the collar.

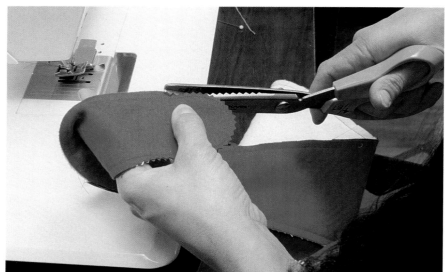

Finger-press the edges of the piece. Topstitch ⅛ inch from the edge around the edges of the piece, using "invisible" monofilament thread on the top of the machine and thread to match the chamois in the bobbin.

## Quilt Osprey Design

Trace the osprey pattern onto freezer paper; cut out the freezer-paper template. Position the template as desired on the collar and iron it in place. Draw around it with a chalk pencil and peel the freezer paper away. Quilt with a highly contrasting thread.

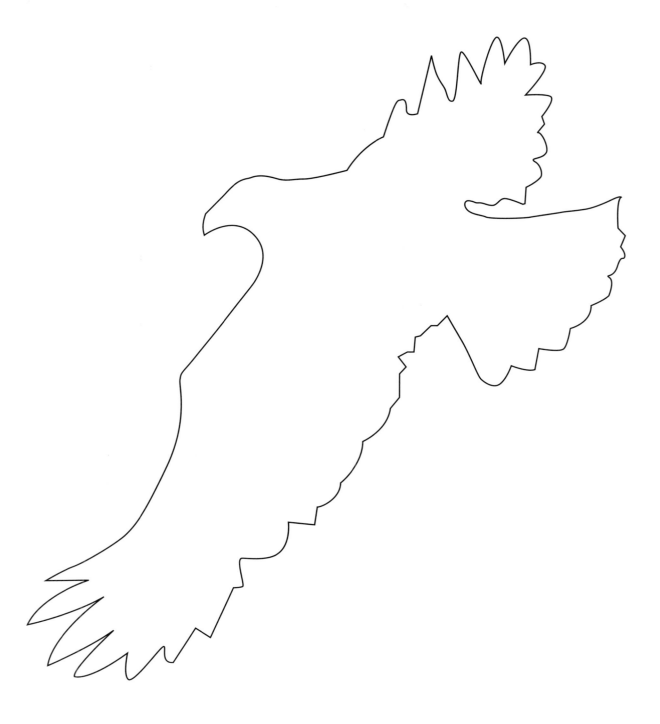

# Up and Away with Log Cabin Patchwork

"Everywhere I go, I see things that inspire new quilt ideas," Flavin Glover says. "A hot air balloon race in Albuquerque, New Mexico, led me to stitch *Chasing the Wind*. It's a fantasy balloon race. You know, I've never flown in a balloon, but I'd love to go. This piece hangs in the loft area of our home and is one of our favorites. It's a kind of 'Good morning to you!' quilt."

Like most of her quilts, Flavin's *Chasing the Wind* involves the imaginative use of Log Cabin patchwork. Very small (four-inch) traditional Log Cabin blocks combine to make an exciting pictorial image. "Traditional Log Cabin shapes work very well in this way," she explains. "I begin with a grid and just work out the picture. Sometimes it's necessary to add bits of appliqué, but in this quilt I was able to get all the detail with piecing."

Flavin has been making Log Cabin patchwork since 1975, around the time her mother taught her to quilt. A neighbor on an adjacent farm, Vonda Lee Waldrep, showed them a beautiful Log Cabin she had hand-pieced and quilted. With that introduction, Flavin machine-pieced similar blocks. First, she made a few pillows. Then, needing tablecloths, she decided to stitch them Log Cabin style. "I hand-quilted the Log Cabin piecework to a backing, with no batting inside.

*Chasing the Wind*, 78" x 92", 1982

When I washed the tablecloths, they crinkled up and gave a nice effect. They've been very durable—we're still using them!"

Continuing to quilt Log Cabin patchwork in the style her neighbor had taught her, Flavin eventually showed her quilts at the Southern Quilt Symposium in Chattanooga, Tennessee. There she saw the work of other quilters, including Mildred Locke. Studying the various styles, Flavin began to understand that Log Cabin could be

*I think of Log Cabin as an American classic. It's such an incredibly strong design.*

approached in different ways. At that time, her neighbor, for example, always "split the logs" or quilted down the middle of each strip. Mildred and other quilters at the symposium often quilted near the "ditch" of the seam. Flavin realized that Log Cabin, rather than being a simple and set pattern, was a design foundation that offered many interesting options.

"I began teaching workshops in Log Cabin patchwork, an activity that supported my research in the area. In working with Log Cabin, I kept trying to stretch a little, and I've been delighted to find that there are so many possibilities. I keep seeing new ways to work with the design, including new shapes to try. One of the joys of teaching is the sharing of ideas and techniques the participants provide. While teaching, I'm constantly learning."

Her first important departure from traditional design produced her scenic Log Cabin quilts, which now number ten. "The first scenic quilt I made was a piece called *Mountains and Meadows*. It was based on a design my husband, Glenn, drew for me. One day he made a sketch for me—just a little drawing based on a slide from a trip we'd made out west. It was a landscape with 45-degree angles and a square sun. When I looked at it, I realized that I could make the sun round by using diagonal divisions of color in two adjacent square blocks. Later I realized that if I manipulated the blocks—introducing elongated Courthouse Steps blocks—I could get other angles in there, to represent steep inclines. So I took it and ran with it."

Working with a basic grid as a "road map," Flavin found that one new design has led quickly to another. She feels no need to limit herself to Log Cabin blocks, but pulls in other shapes, as in her recent work with Tumbling Blocks.

"Today," she says, "we have so many different types of fabrics—that's been an inspiration, too—just seeing what can be done with all those fabrics. Scrap quilts are part of my heritage. Log Cabin blocks, while they are very organized, also are 'cousins' to string and strip piecing. They all offer wonderful ways of playing with a scrappy look. Just the way the blocks are built sets up the opportunity for contrast. When the blocks are put together, an overall design takes over. That's where the tricks occur, the movement. The overall effectiveness of many Log Cabin quilts comes from what happens when the blocks are put together—how the many fabrics work together and how the prints project. Sometimes the most garish fabrics are actually the most effective."

As a matter of fact, Flavin, whose quilt color schemes range from very subtle contrasts of neutrals to riotous celebrations of color, takes delight in discovering the potential of all fabrics. "I don't mind one bit working with offbeat fabrics," she says. "A fabric doesn't have to be 'pretty' for me to buy it. I'm more interested in what it can do for me. In viewing some of my quilts, especially the scenic ones, you have to get some distance, as with a painting. When I stand back 15 to 20

feet, it's often those offbeat fabrics (the ones that may look hideous up close) that make the design work."

Flavin admits that her work must seem unorthodox to quilters who don't feel the same freedom to use a lot of color in one piece. "Recently," she smiles, "someone was looking at my *Tumbling Blocks* quilt in the frame. After a while, she brightened up and pointed at a fabric and said, 'Now, *that's* a pretty fabric!' I knew she was thinking, 'And there are *dozens* of other fabrics in here that are really horrible—why did she use those?' Sometimes Glenn will say of a particular fabric, 'Isn't that a little loud?' and I'll say, 'Yes, isn't it just *awful*,' as I keep right on sewing it in."

Flavin also feels great freedom to mix different types of fabrics in her pieces. Her training as a home economist (which she uses as program director and teacher in a day treatment mental-health program) has included many university courses in textiles, allowing her to approach fabric choices with a deep sense of functionality. In making quilted garments that will receive a lot of wear, she may use cotton-polyester blends that will hold their color well. She might also use blends in a quilt—to retard fading in a border area, for example.

Flavin, Glenn, and their array of quilts (as well as quilt-loving cats Dumpster and Bosco) moved to a new home seven years ago with the completion of the house the couple had designed and built. From the outside, its wraparound porch and many tall windows make it look like a turn-of-the-century farmhouse. Inside, however, it's clear that this is a quilter's domain.

Like the center square in a Log Cabin block, Flavin's studio—a large, two-story room opening to an upstairs gallery—is the room

around which the rest of the house revolves. Along with the custom-designed fabric closet and other features any quilter would admire, the room also features a fireplace and central seating area that make this an inviting space for family and friends. At least four to six quilts hanging in the loft area are visible from the central room at any one time and as many as 16 to 20 quilts (if they are not on tour) are shown on walls and beds throughout the house, creating a colorful display.

In areas that receive a great deal of natural light, Flavin has placed specially designed pieces that can bear the light and will fade gracefully. *Shine on Me*, for example, is a Log Cabin sampler made of six different blocks with a variety of cream-colored fabrics. In a house full of quilts, Flavin says, this subtle piece often goes unnoticed, but she is fascinated by the way the piece changes through the day and at evening, with the light.

"The studio area in our home is important to me," Flavin says. "I enjoy working there, and, beyond that, the studio confirms that this is a serious hobby. When I retire, I know I will become more engrossed in quilting."

And it seems likely that Flavin's quilting plans will always include some version of Log Cabin patchwork. "I think of Log Cabin as an American classic," Flavin says. "It's such an incredibly strong design. Sometimes people seem to tire of it and say, 'Oh, I can't bear to see another Log Cabin quilt!' But the strength and versatility of the design is such that it survives that and keeps right on going. People who express disgust at Log Cabins are usually looking at the standard, repetitive versions. Log Cabin has the potential for endless development that can keep it fresh."

## FALL'S GLOW

This quilt is *not* a Log Cabin quilt. (Yes, I can piece other blocks!) Instead, it's based on the traditional Kaleidoscope patchwork block, and it is my impression of all the beautiful colors of autumn, as if we were looking down on a forest in the fall of the year.

In making this quilt, I enjoyed combining different prints and solids of various color families to achieve the effect I wanted.

When the piecing was completed, I went outside and gathered leaves. Using the leaf shapes as quilting patterns, I started quilting away. Since Glenn is a professor of forestry, this quilt was a "natural" for us.

*Fall's Glow*
76" x 62"
1986

## ROW HOUSES

*Row Houses* was inspired by the Painted Ladies of San Francisco, the wonderful restored Victorian mansions. Of course I took great liberties, taking, for the most part, just outlines of the houses from the picture postcard I used as a reference.

To develop the color scheme, I used a paint company brochure containing a grouping of paint chips in heritage colors I liked. During the time we were building our house, I went into the paint store often, and I would find myself practically drooling over this particular brochure. Finally, one day, the manager just gave it to me! When the idea for *Row Houses* came, I dug out the brochure for color inspiration.

At first, looking at the colors on the chips, I thought, "No, I don't have fabric in all these colors; I'll have to search for some." But actually, when I began pulling fabric out, I already had all these colors in my collection.

This quilt has been very well received and has appeared in a number of publications, including *Great American Quilts 1987* (Oxmoor House, 1986).

*Row Houses*
86" x 104"
1985

## UPTOWN

In this quilt, which I call *Uptown*, I've limited my palette to grays, black, and white, and a few accents of red. There is a variety of prints, solids, stripes, and plaids, all working together. Some of the fabrics have a pronounced texture. The majority of the quilt is made of pieced units that are then pieced together, but, where needed, there is also some hand appliqué.

*Uptown*
78" x 84"
1988

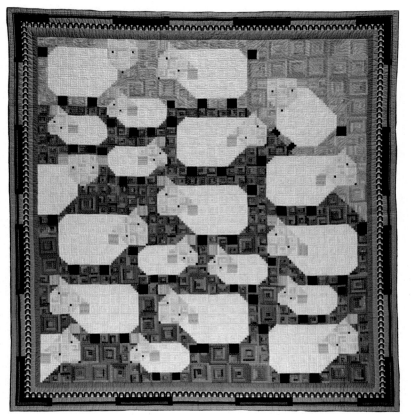

## MORNING GRAZE

When Glenn and I visited New Zealand, I just fell in love with the lambs and sheep. It wasn't long before I was stitching up sheep, Log Cabin style. I first made one small piece. Then I thought, "Why don't I go ahead and make a large quilt for our bed?" Things got out of hand and, months later, there I was—still piecing sheep!

This quilt is so heavy that when we use it we joke of having to turn off the heat and open all the windows. Still, it's lots of fun.

The border of this piece is one place I've found decorator fabrics useful.

*Morning Graze*
96" x 100"
1989

## FIRST DAY OF WINTER

This hanging was the fourth in a series of "farmscape" pieces I've done. All are quilted landscapes that offer an aerial view and create the sensation of flight.

The previous quilts in the series were harvest pieces done in warm colors. For the fields in *First Day of Winter*, I used the wrong sides of fabrics I had stitched into an earlier quilt, to get the effect of frost on the ground.

*First Day of Winter*
50" x 66"
1987

## INSIDE PASSAGE

As a remembrance of a teaching trip to Alaska, I designed a landscape composite using square and rectangular Log Cabin blocks to depict the mountains and the sea. After sketching the design, I "plugged in" blocks of varying sizes and shapes. Earlier in my career, I would have modified the design to fit a specific block size.

A very vivid travel brochure depicting Alaska's natural beauty and array of colors inspired me to make the sky pink and the sea purple and teal.

*Inside Passage*
88" x 94"
1990

QUILT WITH THE BEST
WORKSHOP

# Building Log Cabin Variations with Flavin Glover

In her Log Cabin workshop, Flavin introduces quilters to the rich design possibilities by showing them how to make and use many different types of Log Cabin blocks. Class members are encouraged to experiment with several variations to create their own designs. In comparing the work that results, everyone shares and learns.

In our workshop, Flavin demonstrates how to stitch Log Cabin variations including the basic, spiraling White House Steps block; the triangular Log Cabin block; the square Courthouse Steps; and one of her new favorites, the Log Cabin Tumbling Block. You are invited to use these blocks to make 2 Log Cabin pillows and a rich, mosaic-like Log Cabin Tumbling Block quilt.

## The Basic Log Cabin Block

Of the many variations of Log Cabin block, none is more basic than the traditional spiraling block called White House Steps. This block is built around a central square that may vary in size. The central square—often red or yellow in antique quilts, perhaps to symbolize a glowing hearth at the center of the log cabin—is surrounded by fabric strips or "logs," all of them usually the same width and increasing in length as the spiraling block grows larger. Traditionally (before rotary cutting), the long fabric strips needed for making the logs were either torn from fabric or cut with scissors.

To build the block in the traditional manner, a long strip was sewn to 1 edge of the central square, and the excess was trimmed even with the edge of the square. Then the same or another long strip was used to add succeeding logs, in turn, working in a spiraling fashion around the central square. Often there was a diagonal division of color in the block. In the block shown here, for example, a long, light strip is stitched to central square A and then trimmed flush with the edges of A to form log B. Then a dark strip is joined to A/B and trimmed flush with the edges of A/B to form log C, and so on. Strips of 1 or several light fabrics might be used to make logs B, E, F, I, J, M, N, and Q, and 1 or more dark fabrics might be used to make strips C, D, G, H, K, L, O, and P.

Today, with the advent of rotary cutting techniques, Log Cabin strips can be cut with much greater speed and accuracy using the rotary cutter and mat, and logs are often measured and cut to length before they are joined to the growing block.

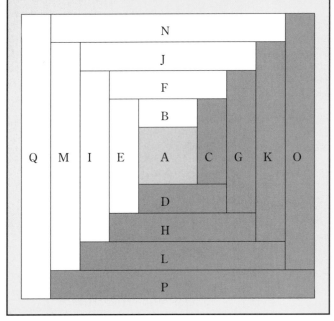

Photograph by Melissa Springer

## White House Steps Pillow

**Finished size: 15½ inches square**

The first Log Cabin pillow Flavin shares with us is based on the traditional spiraling Log Cabin block, White House Steps. Here the color division of the block forms concentric rings of contrasting color. In this pillow, the White House Steps block is turned on point, and the corners of the pillow top are filled in with triangular Log Cabin blocks.

To piece the center block in the traditional spiraling White House Steps pattern, study the diagrams below. Begin by cutting a 3-inch light square (includes seam allowances) for A. All the logs that surround square A will be cut from 1¼-inch-wide strips.

## White House Steps Block

All logs are made from 1¼-inch-wide strips cut to lengths specified. (Measurements include seam allowances.)

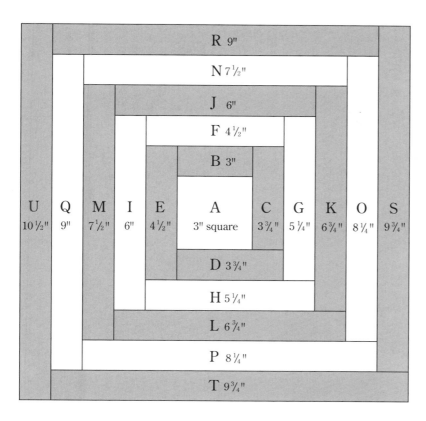

Select a dark fabric for Row 1 (logs B, C, D, E). Cut these logs to the lengths specified on the diagram. Place A and B with right sides facing and join with a ¼-inch seam. (See Diagram 1.) Finger-press seam toward B (the darker fabric).

**Diagram 1**

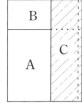

**Diagram 2**

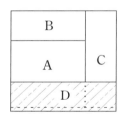

**Diagram 3**

Turn the unit so that B is on top. Position log C, right sides facing, on the unit and join with a ¼-inch seam. (See Diagram 2.) Finger-press the seam allowances toward C. In the same manner, join logs D (see Diagram 3) and E, completing Row 1.

Select a light fabric for Row 2 (logs F, G, H, I). Cut the logs to the length indicated. Join the logs to the pieced unit in a clockwise manner, just as in Row 1. Continue to follow the block diagram until all the logs are stitched, completing Row 5.

Press the block with a steam iron.

## Triangular Log Cabin Block

To make the triangular Log Cabin blocks used in the corners of the White House Steps pillow, see templates A-J found on page 139. Study the block drawing below. Begin by cutting 1 piece A from a light fabric. Cut pieces B-J from a variety of dark fabrics.

Place A and B with right sides facing as shown in Diagram 4. Join with a ¼-inch seam. Finger-press seam allowances toward B. Then place C on A/B unit with right sides facing as shown in Diagram 5. Join with a ¼-inch seam and finger-press seam allowances toward C. Place D on A/C unit as shown in Diagram 6 and join with a ¼-inch seam.

Following the block drawing below, continue around the triangular unit in counter-clockwise fashion, stitching on logs E-J, in turn. Press the completed block with a steam iron.

Make 3 more triangular blocks. Place all 4 blocks around the completed White House Steps center block. Join with ¼-inch seams.

Add 1¼-inch-wide dark strips at top, bottom, and sides of the patchwork block to create a ¾-inch-wide finished border.

Press the completed block. The pillow top is now ready to quilt and to make into a pillow.

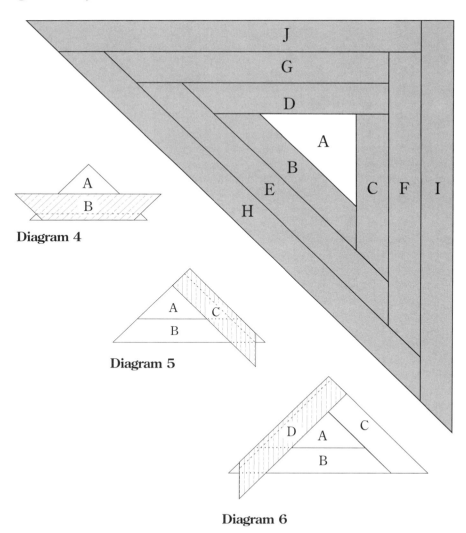

**Diagram 4**

**Diagram 5**

**Diagram 6**

## Courthouse Steps Pillow

**Finished size: 15½ inches square**

This pillow is made from square Courthouse Steps Log Cabin blocks. (On the following page you'll see how the blocks are put together to make the pillow design.)

First, let's study the construction of a single Courthouse Steps block. (See the block drawing below.) To piece this block, place center C and right-hand C with right sides facing and join with ¼-inch seam. Then stitch left-hand C to the second long edge of center C to complete C/C/C unit. Join 1 log D to the top of the C/C/C unit; then join a second log D to the bottom of the C/C/C/D unit. Join right-hand E to the right edge of the pieced unit and left-hand E to the left edge. In this manner, keep building out until the I logs are joined, completing the block.

Photograph by Melissa Springer

### Courthouse Steps Block

All logs are made from 1-inch-wide strips cut to lengths specified. (Measurements include seam allowances.)

| H | 4" |
|---|---|
| F | 3" |
| D | 2" |

| I | G | E | C | C | C | E | G | I |
|---|---|---|---|---|---|---|---|---|
| 5" | 4" | 3" | 2" | 2" | 2" | 3" | 4" | 5" |

| D | 2" |
|---|---|
| F | 3" |
| H | 4" |

This pillow top is made from 9 Courthouse Steps blocks. It illustrates a simple but effective rule of Courthouse Steps design: By positioning a single fabric in 2 adjacent blocks, you can create a circular effect.

For this pillow top, select 6 dark fabrics and 6 medium fabrics. Cut at least 36 inches of 1-inch-wide strips from each fabric. Select a neutral fabric for the 9 center C logs. Make 9 blocks as directed above (see page 131 for log measurements), carefully following the fabric placement key. Stitch blocks together in horizontal rows; join rows to complete the pillow top.

Join 1¼-inch-wide dark strips at top, bottom, and sides of patchwork to create a ¾-inch-wide finished border.

Now the Courthouse Steps pillow top is ready to quilt and make into a pillow.

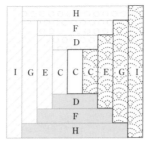

**Block 1**

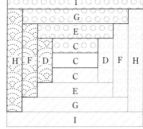

**Block 2**

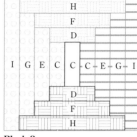

**Block 3**

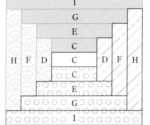

**Block 4**

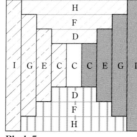

**Block 5**

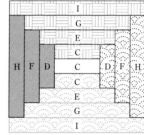

**Block 6**

**Block 7**

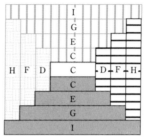

**Block 8**

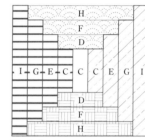

**Block 9**

**Diagram 6**

Photograph by Melissa Springer

| | Neutral |
|---|---|
| Medium 1 | Dark 1 |
| Medium 2 | Dark 2 |
| Medium 3 | Dark 3 |
| Medium 4 | Dark 4 |
| Medium 5 | Dark 5 |
| Medium 6 | Dark 6 |

# Log Cabin Tumbling Blocks Quilt
### Finished size: 87 inches by 113 inches

Fabric requirements:
½ yard each of at least 12 different lights, mediums,
    darks, and neutrals
1½ yards each of 4 different border fabrics
1¼ yards of fabric to make binding
7 yards of backing fabric

# The Log Cabin Tumbling Block

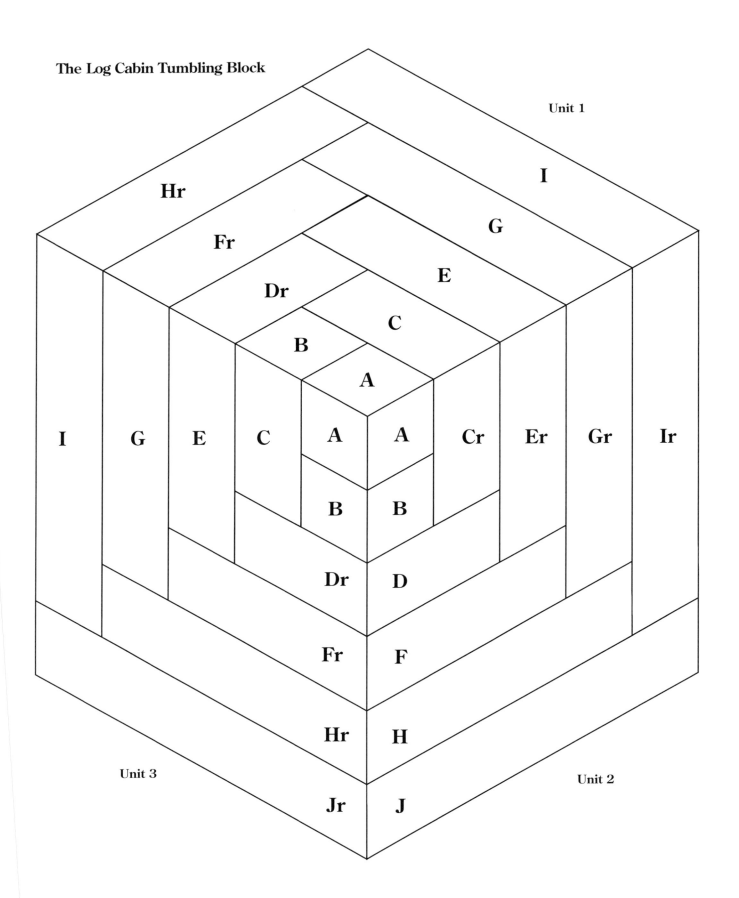

## The Basic Log Cabin Tumbling Block

The basis for the Log Cabin Tumbling Blocks quilt is a Tumbling Blocks pattern done up Log Cabin style. This block lends itself to a number of variations based on color placement. We will use 3 of them in this quilt. But the order of piecing remains the same for each variation. Let's begin by looking at the basic Tumbling Blocks Log Cabin block. (See diagram at left.)

All logs within the Tumbling Block are finished ¾ inches wide. Cut fabric into 1¼-inch-wide strips with your rotary cutter or scissors. If possible, cut the strips parallel to the fabric selvage to avoid the stretch that is common when strips are cut crosswise. (However, when a fabric offers a distinctive design if cut crosswise, I do so. Also to add variety, I sometimes cut a single fabric both lengthwise and crosswise, if 2 different looks can be achieved.)

Each Tumbling Block is divided into 3 units. (See drawing below.) These units are each pieced together separately and then joined to complete the block. (That makes this block different from other Log Cabin blocks that are built around a central shape).

Notice that Unit 2 is a mirror image of Unit 3: Log C in Unit 3, for example, is Log C (reverse) in Unit 2. Cut the logs for Units 2 and 3 at the same time by layering 2 or 4 fabric strips with right sides facing. This will automatically give you mirror image logs. (If all strips are cut with right sides up, you must flip the template over to cut the reversed pieces.)

Note that Unit 1 is like Unit 3 except that it does not contain Log J. The J logs that are a part of Units 2 and 3 form a base for the block and keep the block from being a true hexagon.

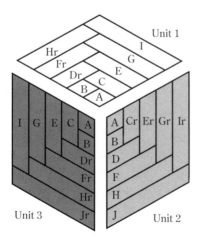

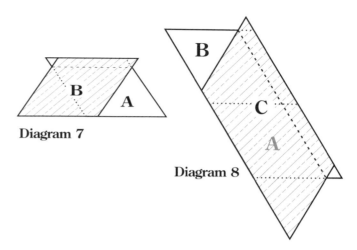

**Diagram 7**

**Diagram 8**

## Piecing the Basic Tumbling Block

This block is a tricky one! Even though I have stitched it together many times, it will still play tricks on me unless I'm careful. To guard against errors, I lay out the cut pieces, stacked in order, along the edge of a full-size diagram of the block as I work. Then, as I stitch each piece to the next, I refer to that diagram to make sure that I am joining the pieces in the way that will produce the correct angle.

Begin with Unit 1. Start by placing log B on log A with right sides facing as shown in Diagram 7. Join with a ¼-inch seam. Flip Log B back and check to see that A and B are angled as shown in the diagram. Finger-press the seam allowances toward B. Then place Log C with right sides facing on the A/B unit as shown in Diagram 8. Join with a ¼-inch seam. Compare the joined logs with A/B/C in Unit 1 of the block diagram. If the angles are identical, piecing the remainder of the block will be easy. Join Logs D (reverse)-I, checking against the block diagram after each addition and pressing the seam allowances toward the most recently added log.

Piece Units 2 and 3 in the same manner, again relying on the block diagram to make sure that the angles are correct. Remember that Units 2 and 3 have J and J (reverse) logs.

Press the completed Units 1, 2, and 3, and join them together to complete the block.

Turn the page and check for special notes on making the 3 color variations we call Blocks I, II, and III.

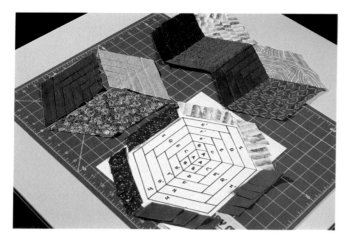

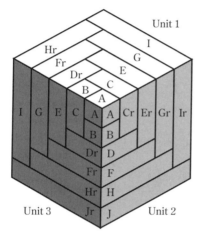

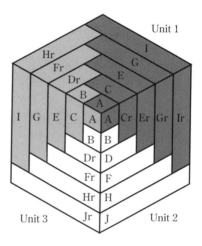

**Block I**

Unit 1 (Light)
Unit 2 (Medium)
Unit 3 (Dark)

**Block II**

Unit 1 (Medium/Dark)
Unit 2 (Dark/Light)
Unit 3 (Light/Medium)

## Block I

Make 32 Blocks I.

Block I creates a strong dimensional effect by using different color values for Units 1, 2, and 3. Use light fabrics for Unit 1, medium fabrics for Unit 2, and dark fabrics for Unit 3.

## Block II

Make 24 Blocks II.

Block II creates an interesting ragged-edge effect by defining 2 color-value areas within each unit. In Unit 1, use medium fabrics for logs B, D(reverse), F(reverse), and H(reverse); use dark fabrics for logs A, C, E, G, and I.

In Unit 2, use darks for logs A, C(reverse), E(reverse), G(reverse), and I(reverse); use lights for logs B, D, F, H, and J.

In Unit 3, use lights for logs B, D(reverse), F(reverse), H(reverse), and J(reverse); use mediums for logs A, C, E, G, and I.

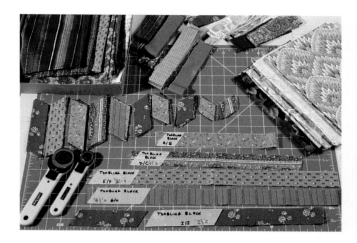

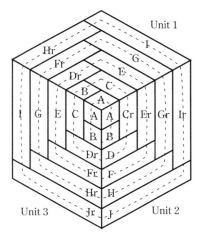

**Block III**

Units 1,2, and 3
(Variety of gray
and neutral prints
and solids)

## Block III

Make 38 complete Blocks III. Make the units for 8 additional Blocks III, but do not join them together; they will be used to fill the edges of the quilt.

Block III serves as a background block for this quilt design. Use a wide variety of neutrals (prints and solids) for the logs, mixed in random fashion. (In this quilt, gray fabrics were used throughout.) In piecing Block III, lay the strips around a full-size diagram and use it to check angles as for Blocks I and II. (For an explanation on the quilting lines, see the next page.) The photograph for Block III shows some of the wide variety of fabrics I used for Blocks III.

## Piecing the Quilt

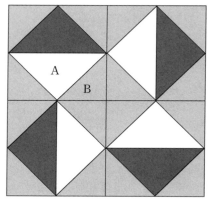

**Border Block:**
Robbing Peter to Pay Paul Star:
Each block is made from 4 light As, 4 dark As, and 16 medium Bs.

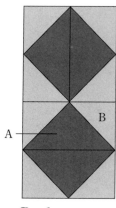

**Border Accent Block**
Each block is made from 4 dark As, and 8 medium Bs.

When you have completed piecing all the Log Cabin Tumbling Blocks, lay them out in horizontal rows, following the sequence shown in the quilt layout. Join blocks within each horizontal row. Join rows. Use the 8 Block III, Units 1 to fill the bottom edge of the piecing. Join the remaining Block III, Units 2 and 3 together and use to fill the top edge of the piecing. Trim all edges—top, bottom, and sides—to form straight edges.

### Adding the Border

To assemble the border, cut the first (inner border) fabric into strips 1½ inches wide, joining the strips to equal at least 325 inches. Join to the quilt top on all sides, mitering corners.

From the second border fabric, cut strips 3 inches wide. Join the strips together to equal at least 330 inches. Join strips to the quilt top on all sides, mitering corners.

For the third (pieced) border, you will need 44 Robbing Peter to Pay Paul Star blocks and 2 accent blocks, pieced as shown. For pieces A, cut strips 3⅝ inches wide (parallel to the selvage) from dark and light fabric. Cut each strip into 3⅝-inch squares, using

an acrylic ruler and rotary cutter. Cut each square diagonally into 2 triangles. Repeat for 176 light triangles A and 184 dark triangles A. For triangles B, cut strips 2¾ inches wide (parallel to the selvage) from medium fabric. Cut each strip into 2¾-inch squares; halve each square to form triangles. Repeat for 720 B triangles. Using triangles A and B, piece star blocks and accent block. For the top and bottom borders of the quilt, join 4 star blocks, 1 accent block, and 4 more star blocks. Join the top and bottom borders to the quilt. For the side borders, join 14 star blocks, positioning them as shown in the quilt diagram. Join the side borders to the quilt.

Cut the fourth border strips 2½ inches wide. Join the strips together to equal at least 370 inches. Join them to the quilt top, mitering the corners.

Cut the fifth border strips 2½ inches wide. Join the strips together to equal at least 380 inches. Join them to the quilt top, mitering the corners.

### Suggestions for Quilting

Within the Tumbling Blocks interior of the quilt, quilt Blocks I and II near the ditch of the seams of the logs. In Block III, use quilting to split the logs and create concentric rings within each block (see the illustration of Block III on page 137).

Quilt borders as desired. In my quilt, I quilted the second border along stripes in the fabric, the fourth border with a cable design, and the fifth border along its floral motif.

After completing the quilting, bind the edges of the quilt to finish.

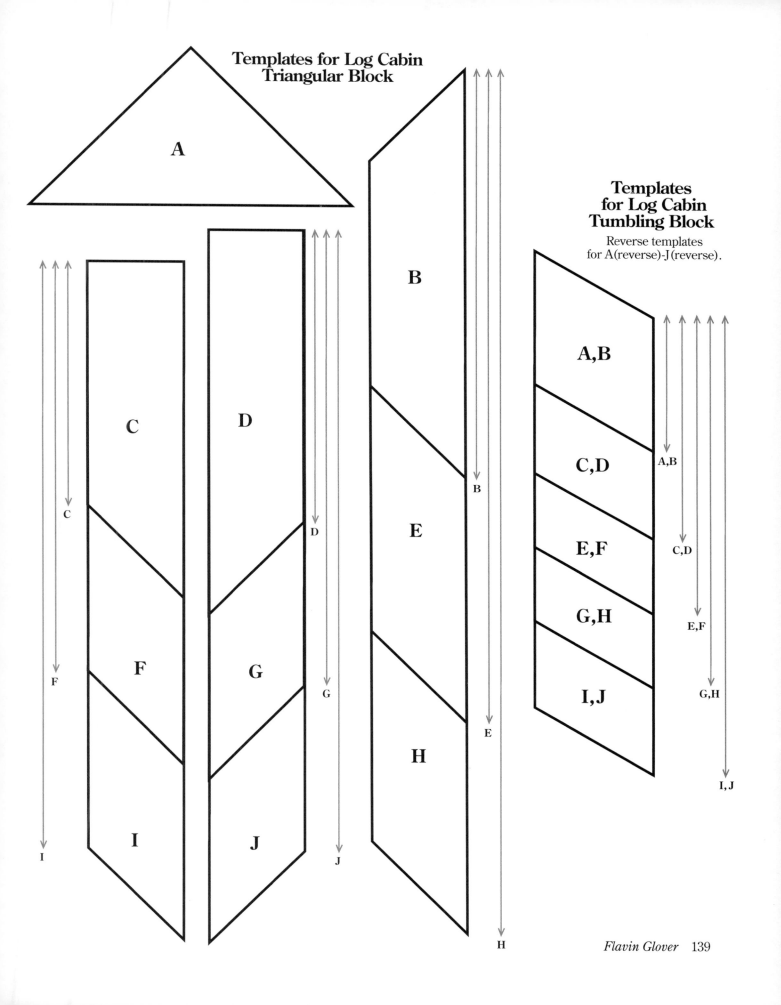

Templates for Log Cabin
Triangular Block

Templates
for Log Cabin
Tumbling Block

Reverse templates
for A(reverse)-J(reverse).

*Flavin Glover* 139

# Art by Design, Art by Chance

Jan Myers-Newbury has always enjoyed traditional forms of sewing, such as making clothing, but she came to quilting by an academic route. As a student in a graduate program in design, she was enrolled in a studio class in color and made many color studies from pieces of cut paper. As it happened, however, the final project of the course had to be made in some medium other than paper. Jan chose to work in cloth and realized right away that she would need to dye her own fabric to obtain gradated colors for her design.

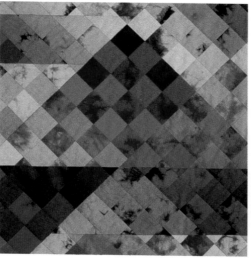

*Tell All the Truth but Tell It Slant,* detail

From this initial exercise, Jan's exploration of color and cloth grew into a remarkable series of quilts that established her identity, in the quilt world of the early eighties, as "that quilter who works in gradated hand-dyed fabrics."

In these early quilts, Jan limited her design unit to the simple square. Working from colored pencil graph-paper drawings, she devised quilts in which colors passed through a grid in opposing directions, creating breathtaking illusions of movement, light, and three-dimensional space. Because the shape *was* limited to the square in these pieces, it was the placement of color, precisely gradated hand-dyed color, that created the special effects.

After her first 120-or-so quilts, Jan began to move away from the simple square to include other forms of construction, such as strip piecing and latticework. In one series of pieces, her contained crazy quilts (see the bottom of page 144), lattice frameworks are superimposed over other design areas, creating the illusion of more than one plane in the design.

In creating these quilts, Jan no longer works from colored pencil

*All my fabric is my own hand-dyed fabric, bar none. It's all the same weight, the same stretch, the same finish—all the same everything. I'm really spoiled by this fabric!*

drawings. She begins by sewing together fabric units (like checkerboards or strip-pieced shapes) and then moves these units around on a vertical surface (a wall that she has covered with flannel), positioning them and repositioning them in search of her design. "It's hardly ever working with this little piece or that, or trying this color here and that color there. Many color decisions were made as I sewed together a block or other unit; on the board, I'm working with these larger units."

Throughout her work, Jan has found that hand-dyed fabrics give her more than just the range of gradated colors needed to perform her wizardry. "People ask me how I can do the precision piecing required by my quilts. You know, half the reason I'm able to do this work is the special quality of my fabric. All my fabric is my own hand-dyed fabric, bar none. It's all the same weight, the same stretch, the same finish—all the same everything! I don't have different weights and different stretches and fabrics that are sleazy and not sleazy—it's all the same."

She continues, "And since this fabric has no permanent press finish or sizing or anything, it's wonderfully elastic. Do you remember the first time you ever set in a sleeve on a wool jacket, and you steamed those puckers, and they went away, and you went 'Ahhhh! It's like magic!' Working with this fabric is like that. I can ease in amazing things and steam problems right out, because there's nothing to prevent this fabric from just easing down into where I want it. I'm *really* spoiled by this fabric!"

Since the mid-eighties, Jan has been working with not only solid fabrics, dyed in carefully controlled gradations, but with fabrics that have been deliberately mottled in the dyeing process. These mottled fabrics, marked by the dye with subtle and unpredictable variations, introduce an element of chance and an impressionist quality to her quilts.

"My work is still very geometric," Jan says. "I don't do any free-form or representational appliqué. But the addition of the mottled fabrics gives a kind of organic quality to the geometry that I enjoy. Quiltmakers who work with print fabric have been doing this all along. I started from the other end, working entirely with solids. I've realized that what I'm doing now is working with prints, prints of my own making. The considerations are quite different: If you sew two print fabrics together, the line between them is much less distinct than if you sew two solid fabrics together, so you can really blur distinctions and get atmospheric effects that you couldn't with solids. It wasn't a planned effect. I've never really specifically set out to do that, but after I do something in a design, I realize what has taken place."

Just recently, Jan has introduced even more patterning into her hand-dyed fabrics. Using a variety of tie-dye techniques, some of which are illustrated in this chapter, she has introduced an ever-wider range of hand-made prints—and, with them, a stronger sense of chance and spontaneity—into her quilts. "The very last couple of quilts really have a lot of patterning," she says, "and greater unpieced areas. I don't know if this is going to be a trend in my work, but it's what I'm doing now."

*In the Temple of the Gods*
55" x 39"
1986

## In the Temple of the Gods

This piece was the first piece in which I used the scrunch-dyed mottled fabric—just on the border. I had completed piecing the inner portion of this quilt and liked it, but I didn't have any idea how I was going to put a border on it or finish it off. It was a few months before I got back to thinking about this piece. By then, I had experimented with some of this tie-dyed stuff, but I hadn't used any of it yet, so I thought: I'll try some of this for the border. I took some pink fabric, scrunched and overdyed it with brown. Then I laid this fabric up next to the quilt and I thought, "Oh, I just can't use this fabric with this quilt: The pieced work is so pristine and orderly, I can't put that ugly fabric around the outside." And then I decided, "Well, I guess I can do anything I want!" And so I did.

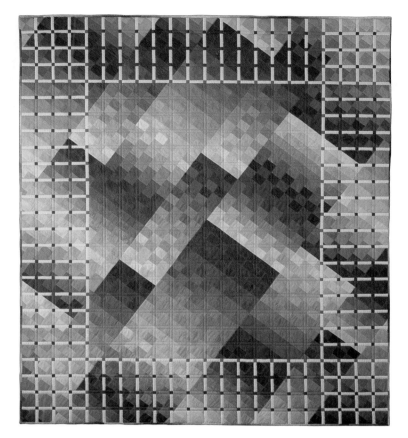

## An Unexpected Pleasure

This was the first piece—after 125 quilts—that I ever used a lick of yellow in. I have always considered yellow to be a really difficult color to work with. You either use a lot of it or none at all. It worked well to just go whole hog. I had a bunch of solid dyed fabrics and I overdyed them all yellow—all the piecework that's on the diagonal was overdyed yellow. Then I just used straight yellow for the lattice.

Between the time I started this piece and the time I finished it, I met and fell in love with my husband. I titled this piece *An Unexpected Pleasure.* For one thing, working with yellow ended up being more of a pleasure than I had thought. And my husband had been just a friend; when that changed, it was a surprise.

*An Unexpected Pleasure*
67" x 76"
1987

## Tell All the Truth but Tell It Slant

This piece started out with the same sort of units that appear in *An Unexpected Pleasure*—units that graduate from dark to light in checkerboard fashion—but they are a little less obvious here.

I had been asked to make a piece for the permanent collection of the university department where I had been a graduate student—the place where I first began making these quilts. It was to be hung on a wall in the departmental offices, and I just pictured my old professors coming to their mailboxes each day, looking at this quilt and thinking, "Well, how did she do?" I thought, "This better be a good quilt!" I really struggled with this piece, but I was pleased with the results.

*Tell All the Truth but Tell It Slant*
62" x 62"
1988

*Jan Myers-Newbury*   143

## SWEET SPRING

This quilt was done in 1989 after I returned from a vacation in England, where I had become very involved with gardens and garden colors. When I returned, I made a series of quilts that are real garden pieces.

*Sweet Spring*
52" x 36"
1989

## THE GARDENS AT GIVERNY

Of course, the gardens at Giverny are in France, not in England, but this piece falls into the garden series. It's also one of the contained crazy-quilt series. I like the way this series recalls a traditional form. In the 19th century, there was a form called contained crazy quilt—as opposed to Victorian crazy quilt, in which crazy blocks are randomly pieced and then sewn smack dab together so that the whole thing is just sort of crazy. A contained crazy quilt has some element of order juxtaposed to the craziness of the piecing. In this instance, it's the lattice framework that holds the blocks together.

*The Gardens at Giverny*
54" x 48"
1989

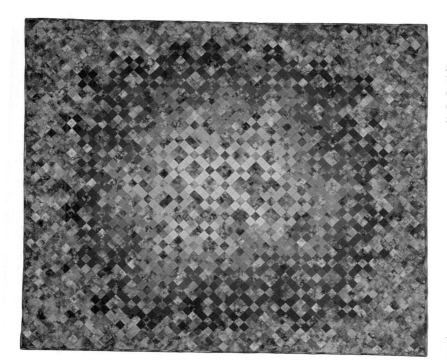

## ARABESQUE

This quilt, another of the garden pieces, is even more traditional—it's a nine-patch quilt. What I really love in this one is the border area—those are one-inch squares.

*Arabesque*
54½" x 45"
1989

## PRECIPICE

*Precipice* was done in 1989. It was the first piece I did with tie-dyed fabric that had a pattern tied into it. The inspiration for the piece was a red, patterned, tie-dyed fabric that I had planned to place at the other end of the quilt. When I added the blue fabric, however (which is cut and resewn to condense the pattern), the quilt top seemed to turn itself and become a landscape. Then the original red had far too much white in it and not enough weight, so I replaced it with the red fabric you see now.

This piece took on a kind of Heaven/Hell theme for me. I had no idea that that was going to happen, either!

Interestingly, in these pieces in which I've started into new territory—for instance, using this tie-dyed fabric—I find myself going back to symmetry to center myself and limit my design decisions. Certainly, there's a sort of power to the symmetry here.

*Precipice*
75" x 93"
1989

*Jan Myers-Newbury* 145

## FIRE AND ICE II

This small quilt is made from piecework left over from a much larger piece. Working in the way that I do (making piecework and then arranging it to form the design) means that there are often pieces left over to begin the next piece in a thematic series.

*Fire and Ice II*
45" x 41"
1990

## TAKING FLIGHT

I seem to do one major piece a year. This one, *Taking Flight*, I did at the beginning of 1991, and I'm working on another one now. This piece does not have much solid fabric in it; so I guess the next step is to take out the solids entirely, which is what I seem to be doing with my current piece. *Taking Flight* also has much larger unpieced areas than I have used before, showing a direction that I'm taking in my work at this time.

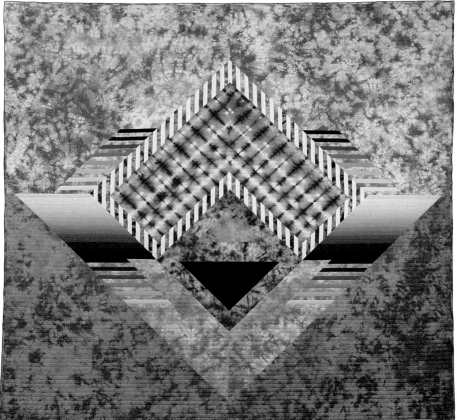

*Taking Flight*
74" x 78"
1991

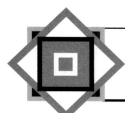
# Hand-Dyeing Fabrics with Jan Myers-Newbury

Dyeing your own fabric in gradated values of whatever colors you choose presents wonderful new design possibilities for your quilts. And first-time dyers will find, to their delight, that hand-dyeing fabric is actually easy and fun.

## Gather Tools and Materials

Here's a list of things you will need and some tips for getting your tools and materials together, including a list of mail-order sources for dyes.

Procion fiber-reactive dye (sources and "recipes" follow)

4 cups of salt

1 cup of soda ash (sodium carbonate, available from dye suppliers, chemical companies, and swimming pool suppliers)

4 yards of nonpermanent press, 100% cotton muslin

1 set of plastic measuring spoons

1 set of plastic measuring cups

Timer with 10-minute setting

4-cup measuring cup with pour spout

9 (5-gallon) plastic buckets—8 buckets for gradated dye baths and 1 extra bucket to hold water for mixing with dye

Dust mask, rubber gloves, old clothes (in case of splashes)

*Tools (spoons and measuring cups): Never* use your cooking tools for dyeing. You will need a separate set—inexpensive plastic ones work fine, or you can use stainless steel, glass, or enamel. Don't use any aluminum or cast iron tools in dyeing, as these metals will interfere with the chemical reactions necessary for successful dyeing.

*Plastic buckets:* Bulk foodstuffs are often sold in 5-gallon plastic buckets, so check with bakeries, food cooperatives, fast food restaurants, and delicatessens for free or low-cost buckets. Various building materials (like joint compound) also come in 5-gallon buckets, so call local contractors as well. You'll need sturdy buckets with good handles; the 5-gallon size will comfortably accommodate up to a 2-yard length of fabric for dyeing. (For longer yardages, you would need to use a laundry basin, a bathtub, or a large plastic garbage can.)

*Salt:* Uniodized salt is recommended, because iodized salt is said to dull the colors (although I have to admit that I have never detected a difference myself). Uniodized salt may be called plain common salt, coarse salt, pickling salt, or Kosher salt. Salt can be ordered in large (30-, 50-, or 80-pound) bags from food cooperatives, buying clubs, or restaurant supply houses.

*Soda ash* (sodium carbonate): The active chemical required to set the dye molecules in the fiber molecules is commonly called soda ash (also called light soda ash or sal soda). It can be purchased by mail from dye suppliers; you also may be able to buy it in large quantity from local chemical supply companies. Also check with swimming pool suppliers or ceramic supply houses. In a pinch, you can use Arm & Hammer Washing Soda Detergent Booster (look for a blue box in the supermarket detergent aisle); but since this is a diluted form of soda ash, you must use twice the amount listed in the instructions for the same results.

*Protective clothing:* Some individuals may experience an asthma-like reaction to fiber-reactive dyes if they inhale too much of the dye powder over time. To protect yourself from this possibility, wear a well-made dust mask when measuring dye powder and stirring it into liquid. Use careful movements when handling the dye powder to avoid "broadcasting" it into the air. Wear rubber gloves and old clothing when handling dye solution.

*Fabric* (100% cotton muslin): It is very important to use a fabric that does not have a permanent press finish if you want to get full saturation of the dyes. Fabric should be prewashed with hot water and detergent (with no bleach) to remove any sizing that might interfere with the dyeing process. Here are some good mail-order sources of fabric:

Glad Creations
3400 Bloomington Avenue, S.
Minneapolis, MN 55407
(612) 724-1079
Ask for #7878 muslin, which is unbleached, nonpermanent press. Width is 40 inches, but after washing will shrink to 38 inches wide. A yard length (36 inches) will shrink to 34½ inches long.

Testfabrics, Inc.
P.O. Box 420
Middlesex, NJ 08846
(908) 469-6446
Testfabrics, Inc. offers a broad range of untreated, undyed fabrics to fiber artists, including cottons, silks, wool, and viscose rayon, in various weaves and weights. Write for free information; specify "Art Catalog."

Also ask at your local fabric store for another good nonpermanent press muslin, P and B Fabric's Muslin 5/8045. This fabric is 45 inches wide before washing. If your fabric store does not stock this fabric, they may be willing to order it for you.

*Procion fiber-reactive dyes:* Procion fiber-reactive dyes are the best choice for dyeing cotton because they are easy to use, wash-fast, and as light-fast as any dye.

*Note:* Procion dyes remain effective for dyeing for a relatively short time after being mixed with water. Mix powder with water to form liquid dye only when you plan to use it right away.

Most suppliers sell dyes in 2-ounce, 4-ounce, 8-ounce, and 1-pound quantities. (As a guideline, there are *approximately* 3 tablespoons dye powder in 1 ounce.) The following is a list of mail-order sources for dyes. (There are other sources as well; check advertisements in fiber-arts magazines for suppliers in your area. Generally, the nearer the supplier is to you, the lower the shipping charges will be.)

Cerulean Blue, Ltd.
P.O. Box 21168
Seattle, WA 98111-3168
(206) 323-8600
Send $3.00 for catalog.

Fabdec
3553 Old Post Road
San Angelo, TX 76904
(915) 653-6170 day
(915) 942-0571 evening

PRO Chemical & Dye, Inc.
P.O. Box 14
Somerset, MA 02726
(508) 676-3838
fax (508) 676-3980

Dharma Trading Co.
P.O. Box 150916
San Rafael, CA 94915
(415) 456-7657 or
(800) 542-5227

# Color Recipes

There are many dye colors available from these and other suppliers. The dye suppliers will furnish you with a complete listing, and—in some instances—a color chart of available colors. I choose to *mix* rather than *purchase* a lot of my colors, because it is easier for me to keep fewer dyes on hand.

The color recipes I use, a number of which appear at right, are built on seven basic colors: yellow (MX-4G), red (MX-8B), blue (MX-R), black (MX-CWNA), red-brown (MX-RDA), green (MX-CBA), and rust (MX-GRN).

Please note that the colors shown are approximate; actual color may vary slightly from the printed colors. Have fun experimenting (try working up some recipes of your own!), and remember that there is no "wrong" color—any hue you arrive at will be beautiful and will be fun to sew, especially with the full range of 8 gradated tints.

The following quantities of powder, when dissolved in 2 cups of water, will make a dye concentrate sufficient to dye 8 (½-yard) fabric lengths in a gradated dark-to-light sequence. *Note:* Some dyeing guides offer formulas based on weights (grams) rather than volume (teaspoons and tablespoons). However, gram scales can be expensive. Measuring by volume is less expensive and easier and, for our purposes, should give good results.

**Yellow**
6 T. yellow

**Lime Green**
6 T. yellow
1 T. blue

**Gold-ochre**
4 T. yellow
1 t. red-brown

**Walnut Brown**
2 T. black
1 T. rust

**Orange**
8 T. yellow
1 t. red

**Kelly Green**
2 T. green
2 T. yellow
½ t. blue

**Terra-cotta**
2 T. rust
1 T. yellow
1 t. red-brown
½ t. red

**Olive Green**
2 T. green
1 T. rust

**Christmas Red**
2 T. yellow
2 t. red

**Cobalt Blue**
3 T. blue

**Brick Red**
3 T. yellow
1 T. red-brown
½ T. black
1 t. red

**Spruce Green**
3 T. green

**Fuchsia**
1 T. red

**Blue-violet**
2 T. blue
¾ t. red

**Raspberry**
1½ T. red-brown
½ T. red

**Teal Blue**
1½ T. green
1 T. blue
2 t. black

**Gray**
3 T. black
1 t. green

**Purple**
1½ T. blue
½ T. red

**Wine Red**
1 T. black
1 T. red

**Williamsburg Blue**
2 T. blue
2 t. black

A ▲

B ▼

C ▲

## Set Up Dye Baths

With all tools and materials assembled, you are ready to set up your dye baths. Cover your tabletop with a protective plastic sheet. Line up 8 buckets. (We show them in 2 rows of 4 buckets each.) These will be your dye baths, 1 bucket for each gradated shade. Set the ninth bucket nearby; you will use the water from this to mix your dye concentrates.

Now place 1 gallon of warm water in each of the 9 buckets. (Water temperature at 95 degrees—almost body temperature—is best. The water should feel neither very warm nor very cool to your bare wrist.) It is very important that the water in each bucket is the same temperature, so set the tap so that the water is just right and leave it running until each bucket has 1 gallon. Then stir ½ cup of salt into each of the 8 dye bath buckets; stir to dissolve.

Wearing a dust mask and working in your 4-cup measure, carefully measure the correct amount of dye powder into a small amount of warm water from the ninth bucket (see Photo A). Stir until the dye is completely dissolved.

Still stirring, add more water from the ninth bucket until the dye concentrate measures 2 cups (Photo B).

Pour 1 cup of the dye concentrate into a 1-cup measuring cup and then into the first bucket (which now becomes the first dye bath). This will be the strongest of the

8 dye baths, producing the darkest fabric. You are left holding 1 cup of concentrate in your 4-cup measure. To this, add 1 cup of clear, warm water from the ninth bucket. You now have 2 cups of concentrate again, but it is only half as strong as the concentrate that went into the first bucket. Give it a stir. Then put 1 cup of this "new" concentrate into the second bucket to make the second dye bath (Photo C).

D ▽

Once again, you are left holding 1 cup of concentrate. To this add 1 cup of clear, warm water from the ninth bucket. You now have 2 cups of concentrate again, but it is only half as strong as the liquid that went into the second bucket. Give it a stir; then put 1 cup of the concentrate into the third bucket.

And so on. Proceed down the line of buckets (see Photo D), putting 1 cup of concentrate into each bucket and replacing it with a cup of clear water, 1 cup of concentrate into the next bucket and replacing that with 1 cup of water, until you have put 1 cup of progressively weaker concentrate into each of the 8 dye baths. (You will have 1 final cup of concentrate left over, which you will not use.) In Photo E, you see the ninth bucket in the upper right corner, and 6 of the 8-dye bath series (the other 2 buckets are just outside the picture in the lower left corner). Now you are ready to dye.

◀ E

## Now Add Fabric

Place ½-yard length of prewashed, dampened fabric into each of the 8 dye baths (Photo F). The fabric should be entirely submerged and evenly distributed under the water, with all air bubbles worked out.

Every 10 minutes (use a 10-minute timer to remind you), rearrange the fabric in each dye bath with your gloved hands; frequent and thorough rearranging assures that the fabrics will be evenly dyed. As you work, you'll need to give each dye bath a good, thorough stirring to keep dye from settling to the bottom of the bucket and to keep fabric from bunching up, leading to uneven results. So dig down deep with your gloved hands and really slosh it around (Photo G).

Thirty minutes after placing the fabrics in the dye baths, add 2 tablespoons of soda ash dissolved in 1 cup of hot water to each dye bath. (Soda ash is necessary to set the dye.) To make this process easier, mix 8 tablespoons of soda ash into 4 cups of hot water in your 4-cup measure; pour 1 cup into each of the first 4 buckets. Repeat for the second 4 buckets. Stir each dye bath immediately after the addition of the soda ash (Photo H). After all the soda ash has been added, continue to dye the fabrics for 60 minutes longer. Continue to rearrange fabrics and stir dye baths at 10-minute intervals.

## Remove Fabrics, Rinse, and Dry

After 90 minutes of dyeing (30 minutes before the addition of soda ash and 60 minutes following), remove fabrics from dye baths, squeezing out excess liquids (Photo I). Rinse fabrics in warm water to remove most of the excess, unreacted dye; squeeze, and set aside (Photo J). Take care that darker fabrics do not touch lighter ones, to prevent the lighter fabrics from being stained.

Photo K shows the gradated series of dyed fabric lengths, just after they have been pulled from the series of dye baths. To complete the process, machine-wash fabrics in a long, hot cycle, using detergent. (You can wash all shades together; in fact, it's fine to wash rinsed-out fabrics of different colors together.) This washing is not "setting" the dye—that has already been accomplished in the dye bath; it is simply removing any excess, unreacted dye from the cloth. (*Note:* If dyed fabric must be held an appreciable length of time before washing, wrap each piece separately in plastic to keep it from drying out.)

Dry fabrics in the dryer, iron, and fold (Photo L). Your hand-dyed fabric, in gradated shades, is ready to use!

◁ J

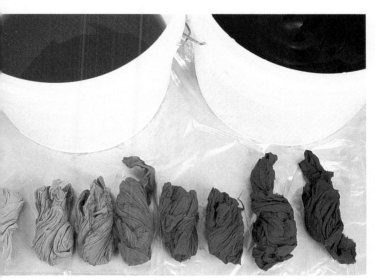

K ▲

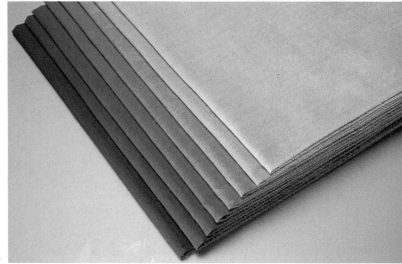

L ▷

# Designing with Gradated Fabrics

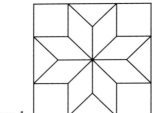

Figure 1

Now you know how to dye your own fabrics to obtain 8 gradated shades of as many colors as you like. There are many ways to put these expanded color choices to work in your quilts. You might start by exploring the possibilities in familiar pieced quilt designs; fabrics dyed in gradated dark-to-light sequences work beautifully in quilts built with traditional blocks. To get an idea of some of the possibilities, study these drawings based on the Eight-Pointed Star.

Figure 1 above illustrates a single Eight-Pointed Star block; Figure 2 shows 4 blocks placed edge to edge. Figure 3 shows 9 blocks, without the lines where the blocks are joined. Sometimes it is easier to see the formation of secondary shapes when the block lines are eliminated. The "figure" of the star becomes less obvious, and the large squares between stars become the visually dominant shapes. These squares can also be divided into other shapes (rectangles, triangles, and smaller squares), as you'll see in the drawings that follow.

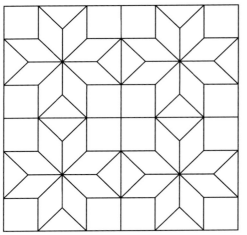

Figure 2

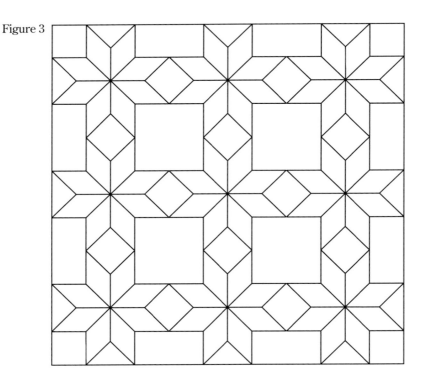

Figure 3

In Figure 4 and Figure 5, we break each of the large squares between stars into a diamond-within-a-square and add colored-pencil shading to show how the use of various value levels can create a luminous effect—and a sense of depth—by the orderly juxtaposition of lights and darks. In the examples here, the lights and darks are reversed. With a border, each of these designs could become a small wall quilt. Or, each grouping of 4 blocks could be considered 1 megablock and this megablock repeated 4 or 9 times to create a larger design. Think about varying the colorways in each of the 4 or 9 blocks.

Figure 4

Figure 5

Figure 6 is another 4-block possibility that retains the lines where the blocks are joined. This leads to the 9-block design in Figure 7, in which the color is varied from block to block. Using the full 8-shade value range in an orderly fashion will just about guarantee the feeling of light in the quilt, especially if the light-to-dark sequence of 1 hue (in each star) is going in the opposite direction from the light-to-dark sequence of the other hue family (in the background).

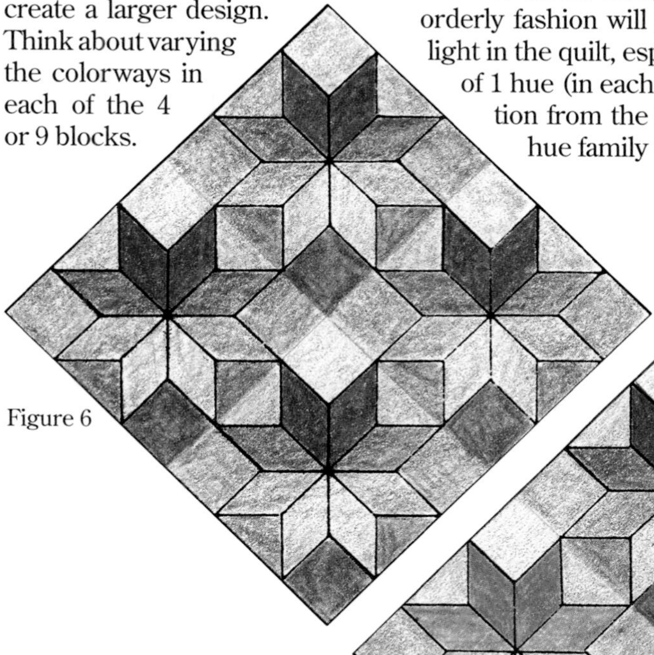

Figure 6

Figure 7

Figure 8 is made up of 30 blocks. Color is moved across the entire surface, not simply through individual blocks. The potential for color adventure is unlimited when you work in this fashion! In this example, the star itself is still a fairly obvious figure in the composition, particularly since a solid color is used for the 2 center stars.

Figure 8

In Figure 9, on the other hand, the stars are broken into groups of 1, 2, or 4 diamonds, and each of these groups is treated as a separate element. Several different color sequences gradate as they move across the surface of this design, and often they move in opposing directions. This creates a wonderful ambiguity about what is figure and what is ground, and we enjoy the effects of both luminosity and color movement.

Figure 9

# Experimenting with Tie-Dye Effects

With a variety of tie-dye methods, you can obtain many patterned effects in your hand-dyed fabrics. Simply prepare prewashed fabrics as shown here (using dampened fabrics, in each case, will yield the most distinct patterns), place in the dye bath, and dye in the usual manner for 1½ hours. Then remove the fabric from the bath; free it from whatever device you've used to prepare it; and wash, dry, and press it as for solid dyed fabrics. (*Note:* In the first washing of tie-dyed fabrics, you may wish to use a special detergent, available from dye sources, called Synthrapol. This product, which contains a scouring agent, costs a bit more than ordinary detergent, but it will help to prevent *back-dyeing*, or inadvertently getting dye into the white areas of your design during the after-dyeing wash.)

One of the easiest ways to prepare fabric for tie-dyeing is a simple scrunch-and-ball technique. Use your extended fingers as shown to "tickle" the fabric into a mass of uneven gathers. Use the heels of your hands to keep the mass in place as you continue to gather the fabric length. Finally, compress the gathered mass into a rounded ball. Wrap a piece of net tulle around the ball and tie it with a string. Dyed, this scrunched ball will yield the wonderful random marbling in the fabrics shown here.

To create this design, make accordion-style folds down the length of the fabric and clip clothespins along the folded edges.

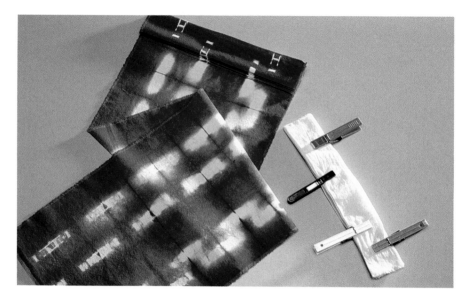

To make this flower-like design, first fold a length of fabric into thirds, accordion-style. Then make triangular folds, again accordion-style. (Do not fold fabric in on itself, unless you want half of the fabric to remain all white.) Secure the folded fabric with string, as shown.

This unusual dotted design was made with a metal C-clamp and 2 plastic bottle caps. Fold the fabric in thirds and then into squares somewhat larger than the bottle caps to be used. Place folded fabric and bottle caps (just opposite each other on either side of the fabric) in the C-clamp. Note how the circles grow less distinct near the middle of the folded fabric. Using a bottle cap on one end only would yield different and probably interesting effects. Remember that experimentation is at the heart of tie-dye, and the unpredictability of results is a great part of the fun of using these techniques.

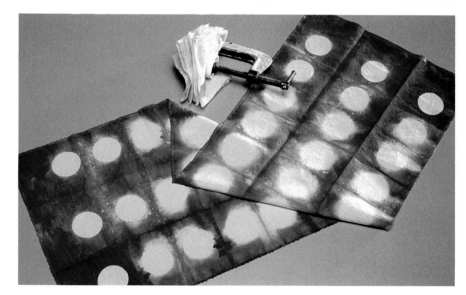

# Faculty Listing

To contact the teachers featured in this volume, write directly to them at the following addresses.

Marta Amundson
HC36-85 Goose Knob Drive
Riverton, WY 82501

Cheryl Greider Bradkin
3534 Altamont Drive
Carmichael, CA 95608

Flavin Glover
861 Ogletree Road
Auburn, AL 36830

Helen Kelley
2215 Stinson Boulevard
Minneapolis, MN 55418

Margaret J. Miller
P.O. Box 798
Woodinville, WA 98072

Jan Myers-Newbury
7422 Ben Hur Street
Pittsburgh, PA 15208

Ami Simms
4206 Sheraton Drive
Flint, MI 48532

Merikay Waldvogel
1501 Whitower Road
Knoxville, TN 37919

*Quilt with the Best* wishes to express special thanks to Bernina of America, Inc., for supplying the sewing machine used in some of the photography in this book.